How Cancer Made Me a Mommy

Aly's Fight to Be a Mom

Dr. Aly Taylor

www.alysfight.com

How Cancer Made Me a Mommy

Dr. Aly Taylor

Photos by: Unveiled Radiance, Angela Groce

Formatting and Layout assistance by: Josh and Aly Taylor

Table of Contents

How Cancer Made Me A Mommy

Hi, My name is Aly, and I am a simple girl, wife, family therapist, friend, follower of Christ, and a mommy- to-be. I'm low maintenance and most often content in any circumstance. I've always found myself to be pretty average and low-key. Nothing too entirely special about me. My ideal perfect day and night consists of a good book, a heated blanket, a Netflix marathon, and quality time with my husband and friends.

Funny thing is, God used *me*, yes, simple, little ole' me, to do something incredible. Something amazing. Mind- blowing. He used me to show His power, His faithfulness, His healing in my life.

Whether you are facing cancer, lost someone to cancer, or know someone who is fighting for their life, this short book will bring you hope. Oh how I LONGED for a book of hope during my cancer journey! I pray it is just that for you.

Maybe you are facing infertility. Who grows up ever thinking they will experience cancer? Or thinking you won't be able to conceive? It just isn't something we consider in our "fairy-tale" worlds! Well, let me tell you there *is* HOPE v in Jesus.

Whether you are believing for a biological child, open to adoption, or egg or sperm donation, this book is for you. I will share some of the hardest parts of my journey of infertility with you and encourage you to pray God's word over your life for whatever it is you are believing and praying for.

I know that God did not have me go through cancer and infertility just for me to experience the heart-wrenching pain that comes with both. I know he didn't have me go through it to just deepen our relationship and emphasize my dependence on Him. I know beyond all of that, He allowed it all to change lives. My pain has not been in vain, and I believe it was meant to change your, yes *your*, life! Please read along with me and allow God to use my pain for your benefit and His glory.

What If?

What if? That is a question I have asked myself many times over the years. If your life journey has faced many difficult obstacles, I'm sure you have asked this question.

I've asked the question most of my life in a negative way. For example, I've asked, "What if my dad wouldn't have passed away in his car accident when I was 10 years old? What if he wouldn't have pulled out when he did? What if I would have spent a little extra time with him that morning?"

"What if I found my breast cancer lump sooner? Maybe I wouldn't have had to go through so much. What if I didn't have to go through chemotherapy? Maybe I wouldn't have struggled with infertility and spent thousands of dollars that ended up in nothing."

"What if? What if? What if?"

As a counselor, I often tell people that asking that question has no benefit. But, what if it does? And I didn't use the "what if" intentionally there! But I think that the question "what if" can be used in a positive light if we let it.

Let me start by talking about you. Yes, you. You reading this book.

What if cancer had never happened to me? You wouldn't be reading this. You wouldn't be receiving the hope and reading my miracle story. What if the reason God allowed me to have cancer was to save souls? What if God allowed me to have cancer to save my marriage? What if God allowed me to have cancer to heal my family relationships? What if God allowed me to have cancer to bring our baby to us?

Wow. Those "what ifs" are what life is all about. Let's start changing the way we ask questions about our life and see how each path, each heartbreak, each illness, depression, stronghold, and pain, has led us to this very moment. My whole story is about the "what if." Praying that through this short story, you will see your "what ifs" differently

Chapter 1

First Comes Love

I married my husband at just 19, and life started a little more quickly for me than for most. I met the one whom my soul loved at just 15, and we couldn't wait to start our lives together. Josh is my best friend. The person who knows me better than myself, adores me, and makes me laugh every single day. We knew we wanted to start this marriage thing as quickly as possible. Here is a little insight into our young love:

> *We are in the cafeteria in high school, and I am sitting with all of my sophomore class friends. We all tell about school that day and laugh as we exchange stories. I notice a senior basketball player in a hoodie with a smile that cannot help but be noticed. Could this really be the same guy that was my first date at the beginning of my freshman year? I didn't notice his magnetic personality and smile when he took me to the movies and I leaned about as far away from him as*

I could, assuring he would not try to hold my hand or kiss me. Surely this couldn't be the same guy. Even if I were noticing him now, I know he wouldn't want anything to do with me. After all, I had lied to him about him being "too old" after our first date, and then a few weeks later started dating someone older than he was. Classy move, right? There was no way he would have an interest in me now. Oh well, it was a good thought. It was fun to think about nonetheless.

Before I know it, the thought becomes verbalized as I tell one of my friends of my interest in this guy, secretly hoping she might convey this to him. A long shot at best. But hey, what could I lose? He probably already hated me anyway after that terrible excuse of a lie I gave him a year ago. I know so little about him, but there was something intriguing about him. Something different that I hadn't come close to noticing on our first date.

I can't believe it! My friend tells him I am possibly interested in him, and he wants to go out that night! That night! Our second "first date" is much better than the actual first. Filled with laughter and fun and surprise that he jumps on my noticing him so soon. That second "first date" turns into hundreds more, as we date for three and a half years as I venture into adult life and college. Our relationship is never easy, though. From early on, he teaches me that conflict is a part of any relationship, and that conflict isn't the issue; the way you handle it is.

◊

I grow up in a home with very little conflict. My parents never fought, and I never really had arguments with anyone, outside of the occasional stereotypical sister arguments. Although this was a good thing, I haven't really been taught how to resolve conflict because there is so little of it in my home, and I am a people-pleaser by nature. So through Josh, I learn how to love hard and to fight hard. Many nights I spend in tears, love, anger, and bliss, as we learn how to navigate through our relationship, both realizing that this had the potential to be something great, something special, something forever.

◊

We are sitting in his vehicle when we realize that things are changing. I am in college, and Josh is making headway in the business/real-estate world. I begin hearing the Lord telling me that I would marry this guy. Sure, it hasn't been easy, but aren't the best things the ones you have to work hard for? I am feeling this confirmation, even though I know marriage is far away. I am still in college, but I know that this is the night that we will have a heart-to-heart and explain our feelings and future plans for each other .

As I get ready to share my heart, he shares his: Confusion of what to do, where to be, where he's going, where we're going. Cue: Aly's breakdown!!! This leads to a monologue that should be put in a scene of the next popular TV drama. I basically (through muddled tears and dramatic gestures) explain that no one will ever love him like I will. Never. Simply impossible. How could God give me confirmation that he was it for me, and him not know it?!? I do every "girl-like" thing in this famous monologue of mine. What would the perfect ending be? Well, of course for him to explain he was wrong and I was right and proclaim his never-dying love for me. Nope, didn't happen. Silence, just wonderful, awkward, annoying, maddening silence.

◊

Well, as a matter of fact, my bawling monologue didn't win an Oscar, but it does help in winning my man's heart. Shortly after, he is offered a job in another state and realizes that He can't imagine life without me (what I was saying exactly). While he was waiting on a literal writing on the wall from God that I was "the one," he realizes that the writing was in front of him all along. He was asking God for something that He already had- a helpmate, a bride, a wife for life. Yes, that rhymed, and I wasn't even trying! So, the man of my dreams proposes to me on February 11, 2006, and we are married on July 22 of that same year.

5

◊

It was clear from the beginning of our relationship that Josh was different. We were different. Apparently opposites do attract, because we couldn't be any more different! I am laid-back, an introvert, and enjoy peace and quiet. Josh is full of high energy, a TOTAL extrovert, and enjoys the hustle and bustle and all things loud!:)

Our love was special. Our love is special. The way we balance each other out amazes me. Josh makes me more fun.

I calm him down. In our differences, we butt heads, but it makes us strive to be more holy. More like Jesus. I had no idea in our young, special love that God was preparing us, as our marriage and faith would be tested in seemingly every way.

Here is a photo from our dating days... In 2004.

Chapter 2

Then Comes Marriage

After Josh realized that I was the one (finally), we began planning our wedding and our lives together! It seemed as if everything I had ever dreamed of was falling into place! I was one of those girls who had her life planned out at 10. Get married before 21, have my first baby by 25, and all my babies by 30. We tell God our plans, then He laughs, right? Scripture says:

"We can make our plans, but the Lord determines our steps" (Proverbs 16:9, NLT).

Josh was the man I prayed for who would fearlessly lead our family. We were married in July of 2006, and life was wonderful. I knew he completed me, and God molded us into one:

"As the Scriptures say, "A man leaves his father and mother and is joined to his wife, and the two are united into one" (Ephesians 5:31, NLT).

I had never felt more fulfilled and satisfied in living out my purpose than I did when I was made one with my husband and got to love him every day, forever!

I knew part of my calling was realized when I became a wife, and I knew fulfilling my other calling of motherhood would be coming soon thereafter. Here is a little about our wedding and wonderful marriage:

> *"Aly, I promise to love you, honor you, and respect you until the day I die. You have already made me a better man that I could have ever been on my own. You have loved me and accepted me in a way that makes me strive to become the man God has made me to be. I promise to protect you, lead you, and care for you until the last breath I take. I want to care for you when everything is great and when life throws us struggles that make our world shake. I promise to provide for you and lead our family in a way that brings honor to God and His plans for us. I will give unselfishly of myself and provide an environment in our relationship and home that allows you to be the Godly woman that you desire even now to be. I promise to be the best husband and friend and to keep "us" an "us" and*

make it the strongest it can possibly be. You are the single most unbelievable person in the world."

"Josh, I love you. You are my best friend and one true love- the most precious gift from God. Today, I give myself to you as your wife. I want to be your wife so that we may serve God together. Through all the uncertainties and trials of life, I promise to be faithful to you and love you so that together we can grow in the likeness of Christ and that our home will be a praise to Him. I promise to submit my entire self to you knowing that you have submitted yourself and our marriage to God. I promise to encourage you and inspire you- to laugh with you and comfort you in times of sorrow and struggle. I promise to love you in good times and in bad- when life seems easy and when it seems hard- when our love is simple and when it is an effort. I promise to cherish you and hold you in the highest regard. Josh, I love you with everything I have and give these things to you today and all the days of our life."

A couple photos on our special day. July 22, 2006.

◊

These vows are the foundation of the start

of our life together. Even at 19 and 21, we mean

every word we say. Through moves, job changes,
school major changes, four degrees between the
two of us, we go through challenges during our
first five years of marriage. Many people ask us
about when we will start a family, but financial
concerns, along with waiting to hear from God,
keep us waiting. We know that God will bless us
with children, and we desire that, but we just
aren't sure for when. We love our life together.
Josh, Aly, and our sweet chocolate lab, Bella- the
best family I've ever had!

◊

Josh and I are incredibly thankful that we had time together as a married couple before we had children. We have been together since I was 15 and he was 18, and in a way we "grew up" together. We realize all the time how special and unique our love is. To have found it so young. For it to be so true and deep. And to prove so many people wrong that young love and young marriages cannot only last, but be even stronger because of it.

Another setback of waiting to have children also came selfishly, as we loved it just being "us". We have seen other families meet a perceived "need" of having children, or to attempt to fill a void with children, and for us, it simply was and is not there. This does not mean we are perfect. But it does mean that we genuinely love being around one another. Yes, we are ridiculously attracted to each other and love one another, but at the basis of who we are is *friendship*. Josh is my best friend. We love. We fight. We yell (sometimes). We hug. We make up. We get mad. But one thing never wavers. We meant our vows. We are committed to this marriage, and more importantly, we are committed to our God who joined us together. Hebrews 13:4a (NLT) says:

"Give honor to marriage, and remain faithful to one another in marriage."

We decided that when we got married, divorce wasn't an option. Think about it. If divorce weren't an option for you, wouldn't you do everything you could to enjoy the marriage you are in? So, that is what we have chosen to do. And the first five years of our marriage were wonderful, with little to no "curveballs" that might threaten our marriage. We were beginning to think that this marriage thing wasn't so hard after all. Even though we worried about finances, schooling, and just life in general, we began feeling God leading us in a new direction. After year five of marriage, we knew it was time to grow our family of two.

Chapter 3

Then Comes a Baby in A Baby Carriage

Ever since I can remember, I dreamed of marrying my prince charming and being a mom (yes, once again the "fairy tale" thinking). I never went through a "gross boys" stage or wondered if I wanted kids. There just simply was never a time that this dream was not a part of me. I never dreamed of having a huge career, or having numerous initials after my name, as many others do. People would discuss what they wanted to do when they "grew up", and I always felt insufficient because I did not have huge career dreams. The only initials I wanted were "Mrs.", and I wanted to be known as "Momma." I felt like everything in my life, outside of my faith, rested on these two milestones.

I desired to be a Godly, loving, selfless wife and mother more than anything else. I desired to be the "Proverbs 31" woman:

"Who can find a virtuous and capable wife? She is more precious than rubies. Her husband can trust her, and she will greatly enrich his life. She brings him good, not harm, all the days of her life" (Proverbs 31: 10-12, NLT), *"She is clothed with strength and dignity, and she laughs without fear of the future. When she speaks, her words are wise, and she gives instructions with kindness. She carefully watches everything in her household and suffers nothing from laziness. Her children stand and bless her. Her husband praises her: "There are many virtuous and capable women in the world, but you surpass them all!" Charm is deceptive, and beauty does not last, but a woman who fears the LORD will be greatly praised"* (Proverbs 31: 25-31, NLT).

Because we married so young, we didn't have the typical pressure to have children right off the bat. Our parents were very encouraging about our education and spending time together. After all, once you have children, you have them forever! So, they encouraged us to wait and seek God on the timing of having children. I was incredibly thankful for that, as many of our friends had lots of pressure from their families of having children right off.

When we had been married about five years, we both felt like it was time to start our family. Even though our finances weren't exactly in line, I was still in school, and we weren't in our "dream" jobs, we decided to take the plunge!

I was 24 at the time, and Josh was 26. In August of 2011, we began attempting pregnancy, just knowing that it would happen immediately! Here is some of our "pregnancy" story:

> *It is a gorgeous day in Orange Beach, Alabama as we spend time with our closest friends and family on our church family beach trip. Enjoying the sun, getting "sand massages" from our friend's kids, and chatting with some of the best friends in the world- it is a wonderful day. As I enjoy everything about this day, I hear that one of my dear friends is pregnant! I haven't heard yet, because the pregnancy is apparently unplanned, and she is still processing it all. Not quite in the*

excited phase yet, more like the "everything is about to change" phase.

As I see her walking on the beach, I jump up from my chair to congratulate her. I run up to her and give her a huge sweaty, sandy hug! I am truly ecstatic for her, but it is the first time I feel a longing for me to have a baby growing inside of me. For so long, we were waiting because of finances, or not knowing if it were God's timing, or just enjoying being married, but for the first time, I desire a baby. I desire a family.

I felt God give me peace. This can't be happening. It won't happen like this, right? I thought God would speak to me in our quiet time together, or in church, but out here on the beach in the midst of so many distractions? But, yep, that's when I know, without a doubt- it is time.

As we drive home from that beach trip, Josh and I have a discussion about trying for a baby, and we realize that we are both ready. He hasn't felt confirmation from God yet (surprise, surprise), so we decide to take a week and pray about it and see how he feels after a week. I pray desperately for God to show us what to do. It is after this week, that Josh joins me in confirmation! So, we begin trying for a baby in August 2011.

My Hubby's Approval

It is funny looking back at how with every big decision in my life, I always need my husband's "approval." But it is more than that. It isn't that I *have* to ask him for "permission." It is that I trust him as the head of our household. I never think of it as asking for his permission. I just deeply care about his opinion. I know that people can get touchy about submission, but for me, I trust that Josh is submitting to God. So, when I submit to Josh, I view it as submitting to God. Ephesians 5:22-24 (NLT) says:

> *"For wives, this means submit to your husbands as to the Lord. For a husband is the head of his wife as Christ is the head of the church. He is the Savior of his body, the church. As the church submits to Christ, so you wives should submit to your husbands in everything."*

He is the voice of reason in my storm. What's ironic is that often times, he is the one that can get riled up, and I bring him back down, but most times, that is in smaller matters. Typically, it is *me* who can get flustered in the big ones. Like moving, or job changes, or CHILDREN! I mean, how are you really supposed to know when it is the right time?!? For me, this is always a bit cloudy, and I just pray that God will direct Josh. From there, I trust that I am walking in His sovereignty and that God will guide Josh. I'm not saying that is *the* way to do it. That is just how I do it.

So, there you have it. When big decisions come my way, I am thankful for God's word that guides me, prayer and hearing from Him, and then always my last check- my husband, whom I trust is hearing from God. Here is an excerpt below of what it was like when Josh and I first started attempting pregnancy:

Tears, seriously tears? I know every website says that sometimes it takes a while to get pregnant, but of course I still think it will happen quickly. It has been two months since we started trying, and my "planning" self has already planned everything out. In my mind we would have gotten pregnant in September and have the baby in

June. We are building our new house, and we won't even have to re-paint a baby's room! We can just do it from the start. Doesn't that sound perfect? But it isn't happening that way. I try to remain positive.

I think every little symptom is a sign of pregnancy. From all the baby websites, I read that one of the first signs of pregnancy is that your breasts are sore. I am in the shower one night, convincing myself that they were sore, and I feel a really small knot. I think it is nothing, but once I get out of the shower, I have Josh feel it. He agrees with me that it is nothing. Whew, that would put a kink in the pregnancy plans!

A few more days go by, and we decide it will be a good idea to have it checked out. After all, both my mom and sister had lumps removed that were totally nothing. I have surgery to remove the lump on Friday, October 14, 2011, and the doctor calms our fears- everything looked completely benign in surgery. We are relieved and ready to continue the journey of starting a family. That Sunday after church we discuss how much our lives would have changed had it been cancer. It really put things in perspective, and we are thankful to know it is nothing. Back on to baby-making!

That following Monday on October 17, 2011 at around 5:00 I receive a call from our doctor's office. He says, "We are in complete shock, but we got the results from your biopsy. You have breast cancer." As I fall to the floor and see the devastation in my husband's eyes, the world stops. It literally stops. What about first comes love, then comes marriage, and then a baby in a baby carriage? What about my hopes and dreams? What about my husband's hopes and dreams? Were they all dying on account of me?

It is after this call, after our world stopped that our vows are put to the ultimate test.

Yes, our first five years of marriage had its struggles, as any marriage does, but cancer? You have got to be kidding me! To go from thinking we might be pregnant to breast cancer? It was just too much for me to wrap my brain around. This is not how I planned out my life! I knew that we can make our plans, and that God determines our steps, but how could this be *good*? I knew I was meant to be a mother, and having cancer doesn't necessarily scream as a good candidate for motherhood. I was confused, angry, and devastated. Would I live? Would I die? Would I ever be a mommy? These questions began to be at the forefront of my mind each day.

Chapter 4

I Wanted a Baby - Not Cancer!

Even though I was initially devastated, confused and angry at my diagnosis, I knew from the moment I got the call that I had breast cancer that the Lord was going to heal my body. I believed with all my heart that Christ paid the price for my healing. I believed in Isaiah 53:4-5, (KJV), which says:

"Surely he hath borne our griefs, and carried our sorrows: yet we did esteem him stricken, smitten of God, and afflicted. But he was wounded for our transgressions; he was bruised for our iniquities: the chastisement of our peace was upon him; and with his stripes we are healed."

I knew he paid the price for my healing, and it was my responsibility to put my faith into action that He not only was healing me, but He already had!

27

As Christ was strengthening me, I experienced the peace he talks about in Philippians 4:5-7, (NIV):

"But in everything by prayer and supplication with thanksgiving let your requests be made known to God. And the peace of God, which passes all understanding, shall keep your hearts and minds through Christ Jesus."

God was surrounding me with a shield, and I had such certainty that I would be healed; however, the journey was not easy. There were days I would wake up and wonder if I just had a nightmare or if this was actually my life. There was a split second that I thought it may be a dream, and that glimmer of hope would soon be snuffed out as a darkness would cover me and I would realize this was real. I had cancer. This was my life. I had breast cancer and really no clue what this meant for my and my family's future.

Shortly after my breast cancer diagnosis, I was admitted into MD Anderson Cancer Center in Houston, Texas and began treatment immediately. The cancer was found in at least one lymph node, and I was diagnosed with Stage three breast cancer. Because of the aggressiveness and stage of my cancer, we had no time to preserve my fertility, which my treatment could compromise. I had to trust with everything within me that my calling of becoming a mother would come to pass- with or without preserving my fertility. I had to believe what His word said:

> *"He settles the barren woman in her home as a happy mother of children. Praise the Lord"* (Psalm 113:9, NLT).

I was given chemotherapy treatment for six months, had a bilateral mastectomy, radiation treatments, and four breast reconstruction surgeries. I lost all of my hair, my fingernails and toenails fell off, I was often tired, and had very little appetite during my chemotherapy treatments. I was in much pain after my mastectomy and breast reconstruction surgeries and was forced to learn many pain management techniques. During radiation, my skin was burnt so badly that it became blistered all over and peeled for months. My body was taking on tolls it was not made to take on. But God, yes, *but God* walked with me through it all.

Here is a photo of my best friends and I during my last chemo treatment :

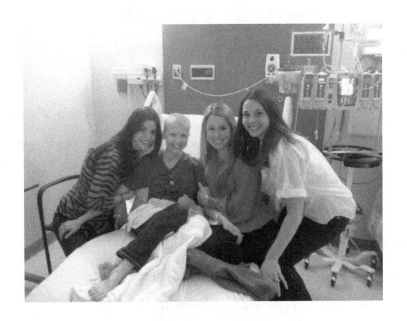

Here is a photo of Josh and I ringing the bell at MD Anderson for being done with chemo!

This was a photo with all of my drains after my mastectomy surgery.

I had to take things day by day. If I knew the pain I would have suffered, the transformation my body would undergo, the sickness I would have felt- I may have been so panicked and entirely too scared to go through any of it. I bet many of you can relate. If you knew everything that would happen in your life- all the pain, the struggles, the tragedies- it would be too risky and scary to take on. But God just amazes me how He takes us through things one day at a time. One step at a time. That is how I have learned to not get as overwhelmed. I just focus on *today*. After all, it is all we know we are given.

So, in a week's time, we went from thinking we may potentially be pregnant, to learning that I had breast cancer. Talk about potential hope to absolute devastation. Obviously, I was worried for my life, but my mother's heart was wondering about our chances of having children.

For a while, I didn't know what cancer meant in the grand scheme of us having children. I was scared to even ask at first. I remember my sister asking me what cancer meant for our future kids, and I just kind of wrote it off. I wasn't ready to talk about that. If cancer meant I couldn't have children- well, I just couldn't even think about that! I just literally couldn't fathom that. Yes, Josh and I had waited to start a family. Yes, we were scared if we would be able to provide financially, but after being a wife, being a mother was a cry of my heart!!! How could this possibly be at stake?!? Finally, the question was addressed when I learned how severe my diagnosis was. Here is as snapshot into one of our first doctor appointments with our oncologist:

"Do you two plan on having children?" These were the words spoken by my oncologist on the very first day that I meet her. My husband and I look at each other and smile a disappointing smile, as we explain that we were, in fact, just trying for a baby. She informs us that I am diagnosed with Stage three breast cancer and that she recommends chemotherapy, along with a bilateral mastectomy, and radiation therapy. She explains that chemotherapy has a high chance of affecting my fertility.

I don't know what to think. I've just been told I have Stage three breast cancer, and I'm not even sure what all that means. And chemotherapy? I was really hoping I would avoid that. And the worst blow of it all- the risk to my fertility. I know I was meant to be a mom. I just know it. I don't understand. I just don't understand.

Before we went to Houston for my appointments at MD Anderson, I had so much hope. So much faith. It truly was amazing to see how God was preparing me for this battle, but I honestly did not think it was going to be as severe as it was. Truthfully, I kept thinking that maybe a mistake had been made and that I didn't have cancer at all! I kept expecting a test to show I was cancer-free before we even started treatment! I knew God was going to use me to show his power, but I wasn't thinking I would have to go through this much. That was really confusing to me. Here is what my oncologist said after learning that we *did* want to be parents:

"I would suggest having started chemotherapy yesterday." As my oncologist speaks these words, my heart drops. The words were hard to get out of her mouth, as she explains many more medical reasons for wanting me to start chemotherapy so quickly. It is surreal seeing a doctor hold back tears. Once again, it is sweet that she is emotionally invested but also shows me that I am sick. Very, very sick. And I have no idea.

But what about my fertility?! I knew that she said it could have an adverse affect on my fertility. We ask my mom to leave the room. Here I am standing. Shirtless, bare chested, crying my eyes out, hugging my precious husband. We pray right there. We ask for God's guidance. For protection over my body. For complete healing. After we are done praying, I am filled with overwhelming emotion. Were we really here having to choose between a baby and my life? This is something that is on a Lifetime movie- not my own life with all our hopes and dreams in front of us! Then Josh looks at me and says, "If I have to choose between a baby and you, it's you."

It was after this conversation, and many prayers with our family that we agreed to start my cancer treatment immediately. The bottom line is that we trusted God. I wasn't trusting doctors to heal me. I wasn't trusting cancer treatment or surgery to heal me. I wasn't trusting in the medicine's ability to not harm my reproductive organs. I was choosing to trust God. Yes, I knew He could use doctors and medicine as vessels to bring about my healing, but if we were trusting Him, truly trusting Him, we knew He was big enough to heal me *and* make me a mommy, cancer treatment or no cancer treatment. I wasn't going to put parameters on what He could and could not do.

And, yes, I was incredibly thankful my husband cared more about my life than our children's lives, but what did this mean for my future? Would I never experience being a mom? Not only was my life at stake, but I felt like a huge part of my calling could be taken away from me. I wanted a baby- not cancer!!!

Am I Not Meant to Be a Mother?

Shortly after my cancer diagnosis, my thoughts and fears began to wage war against me. Am I not meant to be a mother? Did God allow me to go through cancer because he knew I wouldn't be a good mom? Or even worse, did he know I would die of cancer, and didn't want me to leave a child motherless?

There was a period of time after my cancer diagnosis where I had recurring nightmares which would involve a terminal cancer diagnosis, leaving my husband and child(ren) behind, or me just flat out not being a good mother. I finally, with the help of others, books, and therapy, learned to call out Satan's lies! Oh, how he loved to torment me. I would say, " I rebuke you Satan, in the name of Jesus! I resist you Satan! You are a liar. I am a victor. I will live and declare the works of the Lord. I will not die. God will be glorified and by His stripes I am healed." I literally would say things like this over and over and over to combat the strategies of the devil. I had to say it so much that it would come out naturally. I would combat him daily.

I just couldn't wrap my mind around the fact that not only might I not be able to fulfill a calling, a life-long dream of mine of being a mother, but I also was dealing with a life- threatening disease. Yes, I trusted God whole-heartedly, but it just didn't make sense. It even now doesn't make sense in a lot of ways. I guess I think God could have done it differently and still gotten the same outcome, but there is a reason He is God and I am not. As you read the rest of my story, you will see how His plan is always better than my own. But that is just me being real with you guys. Couldn't He have accomplished this another way? That is when I just have to trust.

Through all of my questioning and wondering if I were meant to be a mother, God knew of this child yet to be conceived that He had chosen specifically for me to be his/her mommy. I am and always was meant to be a mommy. As time passed and I continued to call Satan out on his lies, God's truth rang even louder. I am a mom. I would be a mommy. Isaiah 54:1 (NLT) says:

"Sing, O childless woman, you who have never given birth! Break into loud and joyful song, O Jerusalem, you who have never been in labor. For the desolate woman now has more children than the woman who lives with her husband," says the LORD."

Chapter 5

Cancer Was a Vessel

As I look at and read this title, it gives me a bad feeling. All throughout my cancer journey, I had multitudes of people give me positive spins on my cancer diagnosis, and for that, I am truly grateful. Truly. But sometimes, you just need to say, "This is terrible. This is awful."

Just recently, I was able to share some of my old hats, scarves, and wigs with a new friend who was recently diagnosed. I was able to show her my mastectomy scars and reconstruction, but mostly I was just able to relate to her. As we were sitting and discussing everything that comes with breast cancer, I commented on how she is much more positive than I was. She was somewhat surprised by that, as she said that she felt like from reading my blog, I was incredibly positive. And, yes, I was at times, but many people didn't see the silent moments. The tears and doubts. The anger that raged at times. The fear that sometimes crippled me.

So, was cancer a way to tell the life changing power of Jesus Christ? Absolutely, yes! Was it something that completely changed my life and how I live it? Of course. But it still was horrible. It was awful.

I share my entire cancer journey with excruciating detail in a book soon to be released, entitled, *Aly's Fight*, so I am just grazing over the major parts of the process and focusing more on our infertility journey in this book. But, yes, cancer was also a vessel for us having our baby. But before we got there, we went through an incredible amount of pain and loss.

I began losing my hair after my third chemotherapy treatment, and that is when it started becoming real to me that this was actually happening. Cancer was happening. Up until that point, I had felt great, looked healthy, and there were virtually no signs that I was sick. Once my hair started falling out, the reality of my situation hit me, but at the same time, I was thankful to know the medication was working. Here is an incredible moment with Josh and I when my hair began falling out my the handfuls:

"That's just the cancer falling out." I say these words to my husband as he is drying my hair one night. Hair is everywhere. On the carpet, in the shower, on the rugs, in the sink. It has really been coming out at a rapidly fast rate. But, ironically, I gain satisfaction from it. God gives me an amazing perspective of it. It was signs that the cancer is being killed. Ridded from my body, to never come back again. My cancer was falling out, blonde strand, by blonde strand.

Losing my hair was completely bittersweet, because I looked so sick, but I knew that what was making me look sick was actually healing me. Now, isn't that ironic and such a parallel? So many times in the life, the very things we think are out to kill us or destroy us are actually the very things that are saving us. It is through the fire, through the things that almost "kill" us that we come out more alive than ever before. Although most of the time throughout my cancer battle I remained positive and believed I would live, there were many times I thought that everything would be my "last" time. Here I explain:

It's Thanksgiving, and we are celebrating with Josh's side of the family. It is the first Thanksgiving I can remember in a long time where we take a family picture. My hair is extremely thin now, and I am not too keen on picture taking, obviously. But as the picture snapped, I get chills and sick to my stomach.

The only reason we are taking a family picture this Thanksgiving is because they don't know if I will be here next year. I'm sure a rational mind wouldn't go to this place, but from here on out, it's all I think about.

So many want to take pictures with me. I am a celebrity, in the worst possible sense of the word. Everyone wants to act like they are best friends with someone who could die. Could this be me? Could this seriously be me?

There were times I didn't want to go out because I knew everyone would want to talk to me. But, as I explained above, the devil would attack me by this telling me that they wanting to visit with me only because I wouldn't be around much longer. What lies!!! I hate that I allowed him to steal so much from me in times like those, when I couldn't even enjoy people caring for me, as I was believing the lie that they were just wanting to "talk to the girl dying of breast cancer." Gosh, I hate the devil. He didn't steal all of my joy throughout my cancer treatment process, but he sure tried to take every bit of it.

Chemotherapy was hard, but definitely the hardest part of my cancer treatment was my mastectomy and the following reconstructive surgeries. They were painful, emotional, and it is hard for me to allow people to "do" for me, and I had to do that. So there were many lessons of allowing others to care for me during this journey. My main concern with losing my breasts was what Josh would think. I mean, what 27-year-old newlywed husband has a wife with no breasts? I was of course saddened by it all, but more concerned of what my husband would think. I will never forget what Josh said when we were first talking about having the mastectomy surgery. Worried about his attraction toward me, I asked him what his thoughts were. He said:

"I will be even more attracted to you. Every time I look at you, I will see what the devil tried to do, and we will have physical evidence of how God has healed you."

Seriously, is there anything more perfect that could have been said? I do not deserve him. I really do not deserve him. After that conversation, I knew that he would still find me attractive, even though we both knew nothing of what I would *actually* look like when all was said and done. So, now that I knew he was okay with everything, *I* had to get okay. Honestly, I was fine without having breasts. I took longer to develop than Most girls, but when I did (in about 10th grade), I had large breasts for my body and was pleased with their size. Yes, it was sad to think about losing them, but the thing in the back of my mind was losing the ability to breastfeed.

Even though this journey was about me and saving my life, it was impossible for me to not think about the little lives that were lying ahead and how this would affect them. We trusted, like we had all along that God would keep our babies healthy. Breast feeding or no breast feeding. Chemotherapy or no chemotherapy. God is the giver of life and health, and we were trusting Him wholeheartedly for both!

After my chemotherapy ended, I underwent my bilateral mastectomy (both breasts removed), 6 weeks of radiation treatment, followed by 5 reconstructive surgeries. It was a period of my life filled with pain, both literally and figuratively, heartache, incredible fear, and a lot of joy. Here is a picture into my life after my mastectomy surgery:

Pain. Horrible pain. The mastectomy is horrible. I wish I could say different, but it is bad. I need help to do anything. But the moment I dread the most, the moment of truth is when I would see Josh's reaction to my breast-less body. I am scared that this could be the most painful of all.

"They look great." After almost six years of marriage, I am pretty good at reading my husband at this point. The genuine look on his face as he cleaned and complemented my mastectomy scars is one of the most tender moments we've ever had. My husband loves me for me. Breasts or no breasts. Hair or no hair. I know he and God find

me beautiful, and that is all that matters. He kisses
my mastectomy scars.

My husband's reaction to my surgery was just what I needed. After my mastectomy surgery, we had to wait to hear the results of my surgery. He cared for me so tenderly that week as we were waiting for my pathology results. We knew we would soon find out potentially life-altering results. Whether or not I was cancer-free. Whether or not I had to receive more treatment. Whether or not there was a greater chance of my cancer recurring. Here is our visit with our oncologist when we received the results from my mastectomy:

"Have you received your results yet?" Our
new oncologist asks us this question as we are
back to Houston a week after my mastectomy. This
is the week that my husband's faith rose, and we
are beyond ready to hear if I am cancer-free. I
answer her question and say, "No, we haven't."
Where upon she says, "Good, because I always
love to have another person with me when I give
good results." My whole body get chills as I ask,

"They're good?" And she says, "No, they're perfect."

Crying. Wailing. Weeping. Praising. I don't hear anything else. This day is monumental. The day that our faith is rewarded. I am Aly Taylor and I am cancer-free. I am a cancer survivor. I don't have breast cancer; I had breast cancer. Words I prayed I would say and wondered if I ever would. Here I am saying them. I am a survivor.

After my mastectomy, I had many other treatments and surgeries, but the main battle I faced and still face at times, was the battle with fear. I went through a time period where my fear was so crippling that I couldn't get out of bed. I couldn't do anything, as I felt like my life could end at any moment. And, yes, I know we know that it really could end at any moment, but it was just more real for me.

This photo was taken right after we received my cancer-free results. April 30, 2012.

Doctors told me to not worry excessively if I had certain aches or pains, but if I did feel certain aches and pains, it could be my cancer recurring! They would say, "But don't worry..." Uh, yeah right! How in the world do you find that balance of not worrying, but also being aware of pains in your body? Definitely one of the hardest, if not the hardest times for me was *after* I was deemed cancer free. Fear was something I had to fight every second of every day.

When I heard of other people that were in remission from cancer, I remember rejoicing and just thinking how great they must feel. And don't get me wrong, it felt absolutely amazing to be cancer free, but life was not at all what I thought it would be. I imagined that every day would be a gift and I would wake up with so much joy that I couldn't contain it! I was alive! I had breath in my lungs and no cancer in my body! And, yes there were days I felt like that, but most days for about 2 years after my diagnosis, I was scared of some kind of ailment I was having, wondering if it was breast cancer reoccurring.

I would sometimes forget that my body had gone through incredible amounts of trauma and that many of my pains could be a result of the incredible treatment I experienced. But, as a cancer survivor, it is hard to not go to the worst-case scenario. The same things that doctors tell you to "write-off" and that it is "probably just pain from surgery, radiation, or chemo," are the same symptoms that some women have of a cancer recurrence. Pair that with the fact that my cancer had a much higher likelihood of recurring and you got one anxious Aly. To top it off, my motherhood rested on me being well. If I was diagnosed again, I could throw motherhood out of the window, as it would most likely mean I wouldn't be

49

around to be a mother---oh how these "statistics" crippled me! Here the devil was again just speaking lies to me!

The Stance We Took On Statistics

From early on in my cancer journey, we learned that my type of cancer was extremely aggressive. It is never fun to have doctors look at you with such an "I'm sorry for you," type look after reading biopsy results. I was young, had stage 3 breast cancer, and it was rated at almost the highest level possible in as far as aggressiveness.

After those first few days at MD Anderson and everyone looking like I was the saddest case, I made a decision to not look up statistics, nor really ask about them. If my doctor offered them up, I wouldn't cut her off, but I made a conscious effort to *not* know. I know for other people, they like to know, and that is totally okay, but I learned that for me, it would do me no good. Instead of researching, I nuzzled my nose in God's word. I researched what He said about healing. I sought out others who had been miraculously healed by God. I read books about healing. When everything around me was incredibly negative, I began trusting in God's statistics. I knew that His word never failed and He could always be trusted. Jeremiah 1:12 (AMP) says:

"Then said the Lord to me, You have seen well, for I am alert and active, watching over My word to perform it."

Along with studying God's word about healing, I recited a list of "healing scriptures" each night. Along with that, my mother-in-law gave me CDs that were simply songs of scripture. I began hiding God's word in my heart like never before. After all, I was fighting against the king of darkness and knew that light always wins, and I wanted to have as much light in me as possible! I have included the healing scriptures I read each night at the back of this book. I strongly encourage you to read them out loud if you need healing or if someone in your life needs healing. It built my faith. I know I may be too literal here, but God 's word says that faith comes by hearing the word of God. Even when Jesus was tempted by the devil in the desert, he repeated scriptures out loud and defeated Satan. So, for me, to read those scriptures out loud of God's miraculous healing built my faith. And when faith is built, mountains can be moved. Matthew 17:20 (NLT) says:

> *"You don't have enough faith," Jesus told them. "I tell you the truth, if you had faith even as small as a mustard seed, you could say to this mountain, 'Move from here to there,' and it would move. Nothing would be impossible."*

Cancer Is a Climb

It is now over three years since my diagnosis, and I've learned that cancer is a climb. It isn't something you have and get rid of. It is a journey. Yes, I am cancer-free and intend to be and believe I will be for the rest of my life, but after a cancer diagnosis, one begins on a journey that is full of ups and downs. It often seemed like I was either in the valley or on the mountain, without much in-between.

A valley or a mountain. They are the opposite of one another and our lives over the last three years have revolved around the valley and the mountain. Moments of the highest mountains, the biggest victories. Hearing I was cancer-free. Good ultrasound reports, staying in good health during treatment. And moments in the deepest valleys, moments of complete devastation. When I was diagnosed. Hearing how bad it truly was. Trouble with reconstruction. Fear after I was cleared. It can be incredibly tough to find a balance. Thank goodness for Jesus. He is good in the ups and downs. Job 1:21 (NLT) says:

> *"I came naked from my mother's womb, and I will be naked when I leave. The LORD gave me what I had, and the LORD has taken it away. Praise the name of the LORD!"*

How do we find balance, when our life is constantly in the extremes? We must learn to remain desperate whether in the valley or on the mountaintop. We are constantly climbing. Constantly striving. Constantly needing others. Our balance is the climb. Cancer is a climb. It is part of my story, whether I like it or not. I want to share a blog post I wrote a while back about cancer, and just my hardships in general being a part of my story:

Blog Excerpt
November 9, 2014

One of my husband's favorite things to say is, "Well maybe this is just part of our story." In the past 3 years, during and after cancer, some of our biggest arguments have started with this statement. I know, I know, you must be thinking that what he said is a very kind thing to say, but to me, it can sometimes seem like "giving in" to our current struggle. Not fighting something- but just accepting it. I can sometimes hear it as "This is part of our story, so let's just accept this and not try and fight against it..."

While we have battled these thoughts and statements over the past 3 years, I know he is right much of the time. Yes, Josh Taylor, you have this in writing—you are right— sometimes:)

I remember one time last year when I was having miserable headaches. I, of course, was scared of a cancer recurrence. I couldn't sleep, eat, drink, etc... I remember being hysterical one night in the car and Josh saying, "Well maybe this is part of our story. Maybe this is just another cost." WHAAAATTT??? I went ballistic. What I heard him saying was that I might be sick again or that God was using this to grow our story (even though that's not what he was meaning).

When I am controlled by fear, most anything I hear and see can be seen through a "fear lens" which is scary in and of itself. I know fear is not of God and we are not to be controlled by it. Having experienced true fear, I can honestly say that it is such a dark, dark place to find yourself.

When Josh said statements like this, I became extremely defensive and hurt. This often created distance and frustration between the two of us.

I remember when my arm started swelling this summer because of my lymphedema. I was devastated. I had gone two years without any notably terrible swelling, and now I was dealing with pain and an ugly swollen arm. I didn't want to leave the house. It was 90 something degrees in July and I wanted to wear a jacket to cover my big arm. Josh asked me about it and I told him it was because of my swollen arm. He gets on a tangent of telling me that me showing it is a way to tell our story- to show that I don't find my beauty in anything else but Christ.

I remember him saying something along the lines of me showing young girls of how I don't find my beauty outwardly— um, GAG!!! He was so right, but soooo wrong and not what I wanted to hear.

Then, of course, we had our fertility struggles. One of the most heartbreaking things for me has been going back and watching the tape of us finding out we weren't pregnant after our IVF cycle. We had the video camera all set up to catch our reactions of learning we were pregnant. Our doctor called and we hurriedly sat in our living room ready to catch the exciting news on tape.

Well, as you all know, we learned that we weren't pregnant. I didn't realize it, but the video camera was recording the entire hour or so after we didn't find out. Through all my weeping, and questioning, and just a lot of hugging and tears.

When I learned that the video camera had been filming. I said, "Oh, Josh, did you know this was still recording?" And he said, "Yes. I knew

whatever we heard, it would be part of our story."
Gag, gag, and gag again.

Yes, I get tired of it being a "part of our story." Why can't "our story" be one that is "typical", free of sickness, hardship, trouble, infertility, pain, worry???

And aren't there so many misconceptions in that statement?! That a "typical" life is free of those things! So not true- oh the lies we tell ourself! The lies we choose to believe straight from Satan—makes me mad!!! And even as I think those types of things, I know our suffering pales in comparison to so many others...

I, of course, don't know the answer to why we have gone through suffering like we have. And yes, I wish our life was "easier." But I will embrace my story. If I just looked at my life and the hardships we've endured without trusting in my creator and friend, I would literally crumble. Seriously.

I've known incredible pain and I've known immense joy.

It is all a part of my story. Because the pain has been so deep, I know the joy will be that much more. Life is such a crazy ride. Glad I know who is directing it, and yes, it's all a part of our story, even when I want to kick JT for saying that.

Amazing watching and living this story unfolding,

Aly

Chapter 6

Finishing Where Cancer Started: Operation = Baby!

One of the scariest things about my cancer diagnosis were the words "triple negative." This, in "Reader's Digest" version means that cancer is not driven from hormones. There are three types of hormones that breast cancer is typically driven from, and I was negative for all three, hence the term "triple negative." So, basically, they have no idea of what caused my cancer to occur, nor can they give hormone replacements to keep it from coming back!

Breast cancers that are "triple negative" are typically more aggressive, and as you can imagine, this often times left me terrified. Also, those with triple negative breast cancers have a much higher rate of recurrence, especially during the first 2 years after one's diagnosis. So even when I was deemed cancer-free, there were many days it seemed I was just walking on eggshells praying that I would indeed *remain* cancer-free. There were many days I just didn't understand why my cancer had to be that severe- that aggressive. Couldn't I just have had a stage one cancer? I didn't want to be triple negative! I hated when people acted deeply saddened once they read of my diagnosis! That is never a good sign.

But one thought that was constantly in the back of my mind was the thought of when we could start trying again for a baby. At the time of my diagnosis, I was just 24, and I was so ready *then* to be a mother. The thought of waiting for months, let alone, years sounded like an eternity. You moms (or moms-to-be) reading this can relate. When your doctor says to try a new medicine for a few months, or prescribes you an antibiotic while your sick and tells to you take a month off from trying while on this medication- you could burst into tears! That is one less month without a baby! I know this can seem dramatic, but I know many of you are shaking your heads in agreement with me on this.

Then, I got my answer from another cancer survivor on how long we needed to wait until attempting pregnancy. Five years! What? Five years? That was the time that breast cancer survivors were told to wait to attempt pregnancy after their diagnosis. That seemed like an eternity! I would be 29 or 30 and that seemed like forever. Although, I had to keep it in perspective. I would be alive. I had to be alive to have a baby, and that had to be my at that time. So, I readjusted and never really brought up the baby subject that much with my doctor because I just couldn't let my mind go there. I focused on getting well.

Soon after my treatments were through, my doctor started talking to me about my care post-cancer. She asked if we were still wanting to try to have children and of course, my mother's heart wanted to shout, "Are you kidding me?! YES!" Here is a bit of that conversation:

"Well, since you are triple negative, you will need to wait two years until attempting pregnancy." *I had to do all I could to contain my excitement! I said, "two years?! I had heard it was five." Then she tells us that since I cannot take anything to prevent cancer recurring, the timetable is shorter. She explains that yes, those two years*

are more scary than those that are not "triple negative," but once you surpass those two years, your chance of recurrence reduces significantly. Oh happy day!

Typically, a breast cancer survivor is on a medication for five years post his/her diagnosis. It is a normally a medication named Tamoxifen which blocks certain hormones, which often times are the very hormones that caused that cancer to begin with. Well, during this visit, my doctor reminded me that because I was triple negative, I would not be a candidate for this medication. Which, in theory, is not a good thing, because I would not be taking any medication to prevent my cancer from recurring. BUT there is a possible good thing.

Because I wouldn't be taking that medicine for five years, I actually could start trying to have children after two years as that medication would not be healthy for a growing baby! Yes, we knew these two years would be very scary for my recurrence statistics, but if I made it to those two years, we could begin starting our family! Wow—was that a crazy, scary and amazing thing to realize! Two years instead of five- Praise God!!! The very diagnosis that made my situation so scary to begin with, lended itself to growing our family sooner. I knew God worked in mysterious ways, but seriously, God? I could have done without this "triple negative thing." Thank goodness I trust Him!

August 2013- On to Baby-Making

While those two years were possibly harder than my entire cancer treatment journey, they came and went! Wow, was that hard to not wish every day away as my life, literally my life, was hanging in the balance. And of course, my mother's heart was just praying I could get to the two-year mark when we could look at growing our family.

We knew that I would have body scans in August of 2013 to make sure that everything looked clear and that there was no sign of cancer. I was anxiously awaiting these scans, but as you can imagine, those scans also come with great worry which I explain in detail in our book, *Aly's Fight.* Here is a look into the day where we got the results back from my scan before attempting pregnancy for Baby Taylor:

It is August 17, 2013, and it is the day I have long awaited. The day I can be told we can begin attempting pregnancy again. After all, this is where our cancer journey began. I had a cat scan yesterday, and today we will go over my results with my doctor. If everything is clear, she will give us the official "go- ahead" to begin trying again.

She walks in the room and quickly tells me everything was clear. Immediately I feel like an elephant has stepped off of my chest. I don't hear much of anything else she says, as she talks mostly about future appointments. I just want to get to the baby talk. I will never forget her last words at that appointment. "Can't wait to see you at your next 6 month visit pregnant!"

I was so giddy and excited I couldn't even take it. Baby aside, I was healthy and whole- we just had just received more proof, and we were going to make a baby! That had to be one of the best days of my life. And let's just say we heavily began the baby-making journey! Sounds fun, right? And it is, but it also is one of the hardest things in the world. After several months of "trying" with no success, we learned just how hard it is to make a baby.

It still astounds me that teenagers and people can get pregnant so easily. I read every book I could. People would give me suggestions of things to try, and it was hard to not think, "Do you think I haven't tried everything outside of standing on my head?!?" Although, I wasn't too proud to try that. Seriously. I came close to it a few times.

I wonder how many pregnancy and ovulation kit tests I took over our infertility journey. There really is no telling! Each month was a roller coaster. As any woman knows who has struggled with infertility, each month is filled with excitement at the beginning, nervous in the middle, and you are going crazy by the end of the month. I would notice all the symptoms, only to have a negative pregnancy test or have "Aunt Flo" show up.

It was hard. It was really hard. It placed a strain on our marriage. Not to mention the time I had to force myself on my husband after his surgery for his broken nose. But I was ovulating! Whatever it takes, right? Needless to say, it didn't happen, as he was highly medicated☺. It was nights like this that left us frustrated, tense, and sad about the whole situation. I just so believed that God would give us a child and that it would happen quickly. So, when things weren't going according to "plan", it often times left us sideways.

What About Fruitfulness? Wasn't My Faith Big Enough?

Once I was cleared to begin attempting pregnancy after cancer, I was convinced that it would happen immediately. I began reading every book about fertility and standing on God's promises regarding having children. Once cancer was tackled, I just knew we would be victorious and share our miracle once again- a child!

Well, as you well know at this point, it didn't quite happen that way. But it was confusing for me. God's word talked so much about barrenness. And God's word talked much about fruitfulness. After all, one of God's first commandments is to be fruitful and multiply. So why couldn't I do that?!? People always talk about children being a blessing from God. I wanted that blessing. I wanted to raise my children up in the fear of the Lord, but we couldn't make it happen. Why infertility?

In fact, when I was diagnosed with cancer, one of our friends shared a verse with us that we stood on throughout my cancer journey and then as we began attempting to grow our family. It is Psalm 128:3 (NLT). It says:

Your wife will be like a fruitful vine within your house; your sons will be like olive shoots around your table.

We believed this would be me! I would pray this scripture over and over. I would insert my name and my future children's names in this verse. I knew God was faithful to many generations, and I was trusting Him to be faithful to us! There were many times I felt like God just wasn't hearing me, or intentionally holding a "blessing" back from me. I connected with scriptures like these:

"But I cry to you for help, O Lord; in the morning my prayer comes before you. Why, O Lord, do you reject me and hide your face from me?" Psalm 88:13-14 (NLT)

There were also often times where I seriously questioned if infertility was some type of punishment for me. I wondered this often with cancer as well. I knew that there were examples in the Bible of plagues, sicknesses, and even barrenness that would fall on those who disobeyed the Lord. I knew that this was an option and with both struggles, I have sought God and searched my life and heart for ways I needed to repent and change. God did reveal things in my life that I needed to alter, and after I did that, I began to just trust him. I began to trust that He had good plans for me and just because these "unfavorable" things were happening to me did not necessarily mean He wasn't pleased with me. I began to learn that trials come against all types of people!

As a counselor, I counsel families who go through tragedies or heartache, and I rarely question God's judgment, but rather realize that crises falls on all types of people. But for some reason, with both cancer and infertility, the first person I began to blame was myself. What had I done wrong? Matthew 5:45 (NIV) says:

> *"He causes his sun to rise on the evil and the good, and sends rain on the righteous and the unrighteous."*

I had to trust that if I was seeking God with my whole heart and had repented of my sins, this infertility wasn't a punishment. My father in heaven grieved with me over this heartache. Yes, he allows it to happen because He works all things together for my good, but He does not take joy in seeing me suffer.

Struggling with infertility and seeing those who I prayed for pass away from cancer, I often thought, was my faith not strong enough? Was their faith not strong enough? Why am I still here while others have passed away? What did I do differently?

God has slowly spoken to me that just because I did not get pregnant, or just because he didn't miraculously take my cancer away early on, or just because I have had to watch people die who had similar diagnoses as me- that doesn't mean their faith or mine was invalidated. I drew comfort from Hebrews 11:39-40 (NLT):

> *"These were all commended for their faith, yet none of them received what had been promised. God had planned something better for us so that only together with us would they be made perfect."*

And not only did I come to realize that unanswered prayers aren't always a lack of faith, but that our faith really isn't faith until it is tested. It is easy to have faith when something is easy to believe or things are going "well." For our faith to be strong, it must be tested and when it stands beyond testing, it is proved. My faith has been proved through this infertility and cancer journey. Praise God!

You see, I found myself getting caught up in the "rules" of faith. Even when I sent out my "battle plan" emails for our IVF journey that you will see in a later chapter, I thought I was doing everything "right." I remember re-watching the video of us learning that our IVF was unsuccessful and one of the things I say is, "I don't understand. I thought we did everything right." Those words summed up much of my faith. It was following rules and not following the Ruler.

Chapter 7

Our IVF Journey

I finally talked to my OB/GYN about my situation and the hardship we were having on our road to becoming parents. This led to 6 months on one medication and no real sign of ovulation. I had blood tests each month that confirmed this. She finally referred us to a fertility specialist. Yes, that was devastating in a way, but also, it felt like we were taking some very proactive steps in making our dreams a reality- growing our family.

I went to a fertility specialist in Jackson, MS and he switched me to another oral medication to see if that would help with ovulation. Although it helped more than the other I was taking, we still saw little progress. He really wanted me to take an extensive fertility blood test that would basically tell us my chances of conception. I was able to take this test, and I saw the results posted on my "patient portal", which is basically just an online spot for the staff to email you lab results and answer any questions we might have had. Well, I saw the results, and the overall score they give a patient has a range of 0-20. 20 is very high fertility, and 0 is no fertility. I was a "5". Are you kidding me? A "5"!!!! It then explained what a 5 meant. It was all discouraging. It basically said there was a high chance I was in menopause, and the chances of conceiving were low. I didn't know what to think. I learned this information on the day we were moving out of our house, so I was extremely emotional anyway. Here is a picture into this day:

I try to tell Josh about this devastating news, but in classic Josh fashion, he tells me that we don't know anything, and we just need to wait to discuss the results with the doctor. Well, what he doesn't know is I had already talked to the doctor, otherwise known as WebMD! Ha, but seriously, I had to stop researching, because everything sounded negative. This also happens to be the day we are moving out of our house. This is the house I was diagnosed in. The house I was healed in. Josh is extremely emotional today about moving, and all I can think about is this stupid fertility test! I am

trying to be compassionate to him about moving,
while at the same time thinking that more
important things are going on here!

Shortly after our move, we headed to visit my fertility doctor to discuss the results. The news wasn't good. He explained that my situation wasn't favorable and that our best chances of getting pregnant were through In vitro fertilization (IVF). As hard as that was to hear, we knew we had to go home and pray about everything. Because my fertility results were less than encouraging, my doctor wanted to start me on an IVF cycle that very next month. There was lots to think about. Lots to pray about, and a short time line at that. That night, we got home and talked with our families about it all. We prayed about it and felt peace to move forward in that direction. Once again, as scary as IVF was, we were excited about giving ourselves the best chance of bringing a life into this world and becoming parents.

There were of course the ethical issues that come with IVF, and we looked into all of that. We knew where we stood on everything and would treat each and every embryo as the life that it was. We began praying for our baby(ies) who might come from this process. Here we were again about to head off into a very unfamiliar medical road, but once again trusting the One that held my life and our future children's lives in His hands.

Everything about IVF was overwhelming. We had an education class, information to review, ethical decisions to make, and on top of that, we received a box in the mail that would have made us appear to be the biggest drug heads in our city! I remember looking at Josh and saying, "I feel like a junkie!"

I had to give myself a series of injections each day and then after a certain amount of injections, I had to report back to the fertility doctor's office (4 hour total drive) where they completed an ultrasound to see the growth of my follicles (what holds the eggs). Basically, when one is going through IVF, they give you medication that makes your ovaries produce several follicles, rather than the typical one follicle each month. The doctor likes to monitor a woman's ovaries throughout this process, as some can react strongly to the medication and hyper stimulate her ovaries, which can produce too many eggs too quickly. If that were the case, the doctor would typically lower her injection dosage.

On the flip side, if a woman was not producing enough eggs, then the doctor may increase a woman's injection dosage to help stimulate her ovaries more. Also, a doctor may cancel an IVF cycle if a woman was not producing eggs, as to stop a patient from paying a large amount of money, only to learn they could not extract any eggs.

So, there is your biology lesson for the day- The Aly Taylor version- which is scary in and of itself. But that is how I understood the process. So, please don't take my word as truth!

The entire IVF process is one of the most draining emotional and physical processes that there are. I do not know how couples continue to do it over and over, time and time again. We had to gear ourselves up emotionally and had a group of prayer warriors that I sent out emails to each day. We called them our "they" as referenced in Mark 2. We knew that if we were going to get through and on the other side of this infertility battle, we needed friends to carry us and care enough about us to believe in our miracle.

Battle Plan

Here was a piece of my first email I sent out to our "they" when going through the IVF process:

If you are included on this email, it means that I am wanting you to join us in praying for our future 7family! Many of you included in this email already know, but THIS week I will begin the process of In- Vitro Fertilization. This includes treatment over roughly a 3 week period that includes multiple injections, a surgery to retrieve my eggs, fertilization with Josh's sperm, and then a transfer of our embryos back into my body.

After an extensive fertility blood workup, we learned some discouraging news and our doctor recommended us starting the IVF process ASAP, as it would be our highest chance of achieving pregnancy. He believes that chemotherapy affected my eggs and egg supply.

After prayer and much thought and research, we have decided to move forward with this process.

Ever since we felt peace to begin this way of bearing children, God has continued to speak to me about creating a "battle plan." He has told me that we cannot do this alone and that we need an army to be praying us through this process and a level of faith that is hard to comprehend so that we would become parents!

So, here comes the part where you fit in! I know many of you already pray for our future family. But I know that when the body prays together corporately and with the same objective, it is powerful. So, I will be sending an email each night for you and/or you spouse/family to pray the following day.

I will try to let you know what is going on that day with the process and send along prayers and scriptures to confess and believe.

I know this process will be difficult on us emotionally and physically, and I will need help. I will need to rely on your faith and prayers.

I can feel so selfish sending emails like this. But my prayer is that maybe because of us doing this and putting our needs out there, you will be more apt to share your burdens with us so that we can truly carrry one another's burdens instead of feeling "guilty or "burdensome."

"The POWER of THEY":

We have all heard of the story in Mark 2 where the paralyzed man was brought in through the roof by a group of friends to Jesus. They could not get him into the door because of the crowd, so they took him through the roof.

We recently heard a message about this scripture the last time we were in Houston that we believe was specifically for us. The pastor said that the paralyzed man wasn't even the one insisting they tear the roof down and go through it. It was those he was with, his friends.

*"**They** couldn't bring him to Jesus because of the crowd, so **they** dug a hole through the roof above his head. Then **they** lowered the man on his mat, right down in front of Jesus."Mark 2:4 The **THEY**.*

I hadn't really ever thought that before. The friends were the ones that weren't going to leave without the miracle. The BEST friends in the world (which y'all are) are those that care so much about another getting THEIR miracle without wanting a piece of that miracle- what sacrifice!

Jesus will respond to the "they" even when the person in need's faith is weak! He heals those who are paralyzed because of other's faith- wow, wow, wow!

*"Seeing **their** faith, Jesus said to the paralyzed man, "My child, your sins are forgiven." Mark 2:5*

YOU ARE MY "THEY"!

I pray that we can be your "they" for your own struggles and needs. Please join us on this roughly 3 week journey as we pray together for God to do the impossible.

"And the man jumped up, grabbed his mat, and walked out through the stunned onlookers. They were all amazed and praised God, exclaiming, "We've never seen anything like this before!" Mark 2:12

Attached is Day 1 battle plan. I truly believe we will be like those people and be amazed,

saying, "We've never seen anything like this
before!"

  I love y'all SO SO MUCH! Forever grateful
and indebted,
  Aly

I continued to send out these "battle plan" emails during our entire IVF process. It, like our blog, not only kept our close friends and family updated on the process, but it contained scriptures to confess and specific prayers to pray. I strongly encourage you to find your "they" with whatever battle you are fighting.

Josh and I are amazingly blessed to have so many "fight" with and for us. They fought and won with us through cancer and have fought with us through infertility. Cancer is a loud thing to fight. Once people knew I had cancer, the support was amazing. Cards, gifts, prayers, encouragement, money- I literally felt like people were holding me up when I couldn't walk. They were praying for me when I couldn't pray. And they cared for me when I couldn't care for myself. Cancer is typically in your face. And people don't feel bad for reaching out. Instead, they feel bad if they don't;

therefore, cancer patients are some of the best taken care of patients there are. How amazing and how grateful I am!

But infertility is different. Yes, it is much less serious and typically isn't life- threatening like cancer, but it is hard. It is heartbreaking for a woman. For a family. For a couple feeling led to grow their family and not being able to do so. You can be left feeling unfulfilled, hopeless, and alone.

And the support when struggling with infertility often times isn't felt. And that doesn't mean it's not there. Just people are unsure of what to say. How to act. They don't want to put unintended pressure on a couple and certainly don't want to say the wrong thing! It is more of a "don't ask, don't tell policy." And I totally get that.

I know of friends who had been trying for years and people coming up to them saying, "When are you going to have a baby? Are y'all just trying to have fun before a little one comes along and takes away your life?" Although these comments are well-intended, I know they can be very hurtful to couples who are trying to conceive.

But for Josh and me, I knew we needed support. I knew that we could not go through this IVF journey alone. We had attempted pregnancy for almost a year, and with the threat to my fertility through chemotherapy, I knew we needed to seek professional advice. And once our doctor strongly suggested IVF, I knew we needed people to support us. We needed to let our friends and family know what was going on with us. So that they could pray. So that they could care. So that they knew that the typical unspoken topic of "infertility" was not off-limits with us. This was our situation we needed prayer for, just as another family may have another prayer need. Infertility was ours.

I knew that if it were God's will for us to get pregnant through IVF, it would happen! We were praying His will and believing with all we had. And I knew that we were all fighting together! We were in this together!

A New Beginning

So, the IVF process began, and we gave our 5 days of injections and were ready for our first ultrasound. We thought it was no coincidence that our first ultrasound check up was on our eighth wedding anniversary. I got email replies from my battle plan email that day, with many people telling me that the number eight meant "new beginnings" and we were all expecting to see tons of follicles forming, which would mean a greater chance of egg production, which is what we needed to make a baby! I was cramping a lot and often times, that means that your ovaries are working. So, I was convinced they were working overtime!

So, we went in to our first ultrasound check up and before our doctor even does the ultrasound, he gives us the "this may not be positive" spiel. Oh, how we are so used to and so tired of these spiels! Doctors always bracing you for the worst- I understand they have to do it, but we were ready for some good news!

Well, he begins the ultrasound and immediately points out that my endometrium is thin. Apparently, as estrogen levels rise, the endometrium thickens, which indicates that follicles are growing, so initially, he was disappointed. He said, "That's not good." Then as he looked at my ovaries, he saw little to no formation of follicles. You could have heard a pin drop in that room.

I just couldn't understand. I just didn't understand. We prayed. We believed. I spoke God's word. I knew it was His will to give us children. Why isn't this happening?!

Of course, I always have to find something positive. Josh could tell I was on the verge of tears, but I was saying things like, "But there are follicles there, right?" The doctor answered reluctantly that there were a few but nothing substantial. The typical 27-year-old would have had several that were growing and mine were not. He then asked us to meet him in his office to discuss what we would do from there.

Hint #1- this is not good. We have learned, anytime a doctor asks you to meet them in their office after some kind of test result, usually the result is not a good one. He explained to us that because of there being little to no follicle growth that we need to consider canceling our IVF cycle. At that point, we had spent around $8,000 and the entire process was going to take around $20,000, so if we stopped our cycle we could conserve a good amount of money. Here is the "battle plan" email I sent out from the day before our ultrasound:

Battle Plan Day 9 Monday, July 22, 2014
8 Years of Marriage= New Beginnings, a New Creation!

I am really excited for today! As soon as Josh gets done with Warrior Camp this morning, we will head to Jackson. My appointment is at 9:30. I will have an ultrasound, along with some blood work to check on my progress.

This is a huge day! We will monitor how I am responding to my injections. My prayer is that I am responding better than they ever expected with lots of follicles and lots of eggs growing! It is also in this appointment where they will decide my future course of treatment (how many more medications, egg retrieval dates, etc.)

I got two separate messages yesterday from 2 dear friends saying they felt led to look up and share what the number 8 meant (it being our 8 year anni today). 8 means a new beginning, a new creation.

Fitting, huh? I love when God sends me reminders...

And here is the email I sent out the following day, after we learned of our discouraging ultrasound after my first 5 injections of IVF:

Battle Plan Day 10
Monday, July 23, 2014 Discouraging News= A Good Day

Well, yesterday was not what we had hoped for. Through my ultrasound, my doctor was unhappy about the follicles developing. It still is really early to see much, but he saw 4 follicles on my left and one on my right. It was after this ultrasound that he basically had the conversation with us that cancelling my IVF might be the best option.

He said that we were waiting on my blood results (my estrogen levels), as they were a better indication of my follicular development. He wanted to see the levels at least above 50. He said if it was below, we needed to discuss what we were going to do with this cycle.

Josh and I were of course devastated, but we really do have peace. We had to wait all day to get my estrogen levels back, and we had several great conversations. We realized that yesterday was a GOOD day. We were having an ultrasound and discussing ways to grow our family- 2 1/2 years ago, we weren't sure I'd be here to have these conversations, hence the GOOD day.

The GOOD news is that my estrogen level came back at 46 (which is still low), but my doctor said for us to continue on with my injections and we would have another follow-up ultrasound on Friday. That is an answered prayer in and of itself. Breaking statistics once again.

After our conversation yesterday, I assume he was fully preparing to call me to tell me his recommendation of cancelling this IVF cycle and moving on to egg donation, embryo donation, or adoption, but God came through. I am grateful.

As I read this email back in hindsight, I can just hear myself trying to find something positive, anything positive out of this appointment! Looking back, it was anything but a positive ultrasound, but I had to find some kind of silver lining. I knew God was up to something, but I hadn't a clue what it was! All I wanted to give was news of a miracle. Knowing that our baby was forming! This was not what we wanted to hear. What about new beginnings? What about the best anniversary present we could imagine? Not how I thought the day would go. We left with him telling us to think about everything as we waited to get the blood work back that would further indicate whether it was wise to completely cancel my IVF cycle.

We spent the whole drive home, much of the 2-hour drive in silence. We held hands and knew that if we uttered a word, the rivers would overflow and it could be a weep fest on the way home. Josh spoke first, which is very un- typical☺.

He first professed his love for me. He reassured me that this wasn't my fault. Through tears he explained that even if we never had children, he would be happy. I was enough. We were enough. God was enough. We didn't need a child to have a family. Yes, we could have started talking about our options, but he got to the root of it- guilt. He was really addressing my guilt.

Yes, guilt. This guilt that I have felt since I was diagnosed with cancer. Guilt that he had to go through cancer with his wife of five years. Guilt that he was married to someone who had her breasts removed. Guilt of not possibly being able to give him children. But on this day, his love and reassurance on this eighth year of our marriage was the best gift he could have given me. He gave me the permission to be free of guilt. Christ had already freed me of this on the cross, but it was on this day, July 22, 2014, that I felt a peace rush over me, and I let go of guilt.

We decided in the car on our way home that we were going to proceed with this cycle of IVF. No matter what the doctor called and told us from that blood report, we were moving forward. We were putting our faith in this and finishing what we started.

Little IVF Miracles

From this point forward, every piece of our IVF journey was a miracle. We went back for our next ultrasound checkup and everything changed. There were follicles growing. My endometrium looked "beautiful" in the words of my doctor. My doctor was shocked, surprised and encouraged with each visit.

Every time our doctor would brace us and say, "We may not be able to retrieve eggs," or "We may not be able to have your egg and sperm form an embryo." But we just kept trusting. We had to follow it through. We were able have the egg retrieval! We were praying for 1 good egg. And we not only got one good egg, but we retrieved two! Yes, two were retrieved! Praise Jesus! We also learned that night that both eggs were fertilized with Josh's sperm. A day later we learned that both became embryos! We were actually going to be able to transfer an embryo into my body! Everything the doctor warned us against not happening was happening indeed. This could be our new beginning.

We got a call on our way to Jackson that one of our embryos did not make it to the next stage, which in scientific terms is referred to as a blastocyst, but in our terms just means that the baby made it to the next stage of development. We were heartbroken. To us, it was a baby from the moment our sperm and egg met. But at the same time, we were still incredibly thankful that we had an embryo to transfer at all. But there was grieving that took place from losing that little life.

The embryo transfer process was rather anti-climactic as I was put under for the egg retrieval, but for the transfer, it was fairly quick, and I was awake during it all.

Some pictures after our embryo transfer

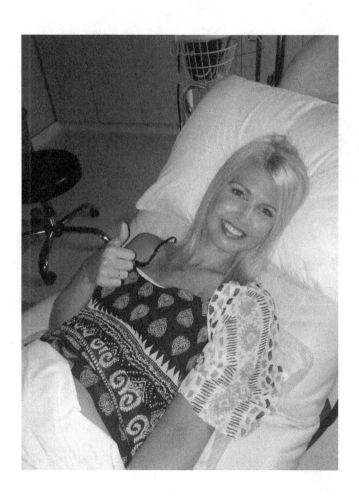

Then, we had to go home and wait for a week for our pregnancy blood test. Hello, waiting! Something we are all too familiar with. Here is a short piece of us waiting on that day:

It is August 18, 2014, and I cannot do anything today. Today is the day we find out if we are pregnant. Scratch that. We find out we ARE pregnant. We just believe it. We have had so many prayings for us. So many believing with us. This is just going to be another miracle in our life. I just know it.

Everyone is posting ALS Ice Bucket Challenge videos on social media and I watch them all day to try and get my mind off of the possible call. I have the video camera set up, to be ready at anytime to catch mine and Josh's ecstatic reactions. Phone rings, heart drops, oh, it's just my mom. Breathe, Aly, breathe.

Back to waiting on the call. I see it is a Jackson, MS number. I grab Josh, put the video camera on "record" and answer the call that will change our lives forever. "Hello" I say expecting to hear my nurses happy, sweet voice saying ,

"Congratulations!" Instead I hear the voice of my doctor. Bad sign #1. He regretfully says, "I'm so sorry. You're not pregnant." One of the most heartbreaking things for me to go back and watch is the video of us finding out that we weren't pregnant. As you read above, we had pressed "record" on our video camera before we

93

answered the call, so the video camera got the phone call and everything thereafter. Lots of tears, lots of hugs, and lots of silence. I mean, what do you say? I was confused. I kept saying that I was so confused. Yes, we had spent $20,000. Yes, we knew it was for sure. The blood test was correct. We were just confused because we just chose to believe this was it.

Any bad news call is bad, no doubt about it, but when you are preparing for a life-changing exciting call and it is a devastating one, it is just 100 times worse. We asked our family to believe with us. We asked them to not talk about egg donation, or sperm donation, or even adoption during our IVF journey. Not that we didn't want to try those options, but we wanted to build our faith. At that moment in time, we were believing for me to get pregnant and wanted to focus on that. If we felt God leading us in a different direction, then at that time, we would put our faith in that. We all put our faith in that. I relied on my "they". I thought I had done everything "right." Then, why did we end up not pregnant? I didn't understand. So many thoughts ran through my mind.

Would I ever be a mother? Maybe this is God telling me I shouldn't be one. Do I need to try to be a mother by another route? And if so, how? The questions that were posed after our IVF journey were confusing and brought up many thoughts and emotions in me that were difficult to wade through. Even though God was helping me through my guilt of what my "issues" had drug my husband through over the past three years, I still struggled with just the reality of the situation, and it affected our marriage.

I Can't Give My Husband Babies

As a family counselor, I have seen many couples over a variety of different issues and struggles. We all have also watched many TV dramas where couples split up over rather large issues and petty ones as well. But I bet we can all remember a book or television show where a husband left a wife because she could not give him children. After all, many of us are familiar with Abraham and Sarah in the Bible. When she couldn't give him children, Hagar stepped in to give them to him! If you are a couple that went into a marriage wanting children, it can be scary when you are having trouble having them.

Especially when you learn the "problem" is you. I would often think and sometimes verbalize (unwisely) that if Josh had just married the "right" woman, he would be a dad.

I am thankful that Josh always viewed infertility as "our" problem. He still says to this day, "It might be me," even though every test has been contrary to that. Even though I know by medical standards that I am reason we have not been able to conceive, by Josh viewing this as "our" problem, has helped me immensely. Any guilt or shame or inadequacy has totally been self-imposed, and from talking to other couples who struggle with infertility, that is the exception to the rule. Josh Taylor has been exceptional at making me feel loved throughout this infertility process. But I know you may be in another boat entirely. I encourage you to seek counsel and be honest and open with your spouse.

Infertility is filled with emotions, and rarely do couples experience the same emotions at the same time. And I hate that Hollywood and fairy tales present it that way.

Very few times are Josh and I feeling the same emotion at the same time. Typically when he really wants to talk about something specific, I may not want to and vice versa. That's just the way it is. But that is a parallel of grief in infertility, and honestly grief in everything. After eight and a half years of marriage, I am finally learning to stop trying to get Josh to do things "my way." Yes, my way may be the best way or the most efficient way (of course), but that does not mean it is *the* way or the *best* way. Ouch. It really hurt to write that. The ironic thing is that when I stop trying to push Josh to be like me, he actually does do things more as I would do them. The pressure is off, and he is able to have freedom. Grieving is similar. We all do it in different ways. Some people cry. Others clam up. Some get mad. Some want to talk about it, and others want to act like their struggle doesn't exist. Josh and I dealt with infertility differently. Very differently.

I wanted to talk about it a lot. After all, it was on my mind 24/7. Josh would sometimes get overwhelmed and have to tell me to stop. I eventually got to the point (well, kind of) where I could not take offense to that and just know he needed a break from baby talk. We had to be vulnerable with one another and compensate for our "grieving" infertility while balancing baby talk and the way we were going to grow our family.

Just as I learned in cancer, Josh hates, and I mean absolutely hates, when he can't prevent my pain. He couldn't stop cancer. He couldn't stop other people around us from having children. He couldn't help our infertility issues, and that was extremely hard on him. It often led us in weird emotional places where we couldn't comfort each other, as we both weren't emotionally healthy enough at the thime to offer the right comfort or advice.

There were times where I would feel like the worst wife ever, as I would gain some sort of satisfaction from seeing him torn up during our infertility. And then the next day I would be in tears thinking that my inability to give him children was what was causing him to be distressed. One moment happy to see him grieve and the next minute feeling hopeless, and I was the one causing him this grief.

Cancer and infertility have made us grieve *together*. They have made us experience a level of pain together we could never wish on any couple. They have made us have conversations that I never imagined in my wildest dreams I would have. All the way from my funeral to if we didn't have children, to stillborn births, to children with disabilities. But it has made us experience an intimacy so deep that I wonder if can be reached without going through such valleys. Josh's attitude of facing this as "our" battle made all the difference. We are truly one flesh and I am beyond thankful my husband believes that and lives it out. Genesis 2:23 says,

"The man said, "This is now bone of my bones and flesh of my flesh; she shall be called 'woman,' for she was taken out of man."

I am incredibly thankful that God bound us together. Through all the fears, doubts, heartbreaks and trials we have undergone, God has made us strong. He has given us a bond that I don't know if would have ever been possible without these struggles. And now that some of this is in hindsight, we are starting to see how through these rough waters, individually and as a couple, He was leading us to something so exciting, so miraculous- that we would never have seen or imagined in the middle of our storms.

Chapter 8

Things They Don't Tell You About Infertility

I Just Want to be Boring Mom.

I knew that this was "a part of our story" to quote Josh, but I didn't want to be infertile! I was tired of having ministries come out of everything! I have heard the saying, "Out of your greatest hurt comes your greatest ministry." Yes, I am grateful for our cancer ministry, but I am tired of ministries! I'm tired of hurts! I didn't want to deal with infertility, or even have an infertility ministry. I just want to be a boring wife and mom! That is all I want.

This road of childlessness is a lonely road and one I did not choose to walk. I often fought it with all I had. Although the process of not getting pregnant is referred to as "infertility", I was determined I would not be labeled as "infertile." Even as I use that word now to describe my situation, I still believe that I am fertile, and

God is choosing to close my womb, either for a time or forever. I trust His judgment. I just can't let my mind believe that is true. The "infertile" term. Although the journey was filled with discouragement, there were moments where my aching soul could draw comfort knowing that God set out this course for my life before I took my first breath. Before my babies took their first breath. Although there were moments where I wanted to throw my hands up, scream, and cry (and moments I actually did do this), there was hope, even in my barrenness.

To really tap into hope and believe God that I would become a mother, I had to give up control. I had to surrender. There has been so much of my life that has been out of my control. It all really is out of our control, isn't it? But for me, with both cancer and infertility, I felt helpless. The only thing I could control was my outlook, and there were really only two ways to approach my devastating situations. I could be bitter, which I know leads to self- destruction, or I could have hope and joy, knowing that produced growth and peace. I chose and continue to choose the latter. As I continued to choose hope, bitterness began to leave, and peace filled my heart as I relinquished control.

There were times I questioned if my longing for a baby meant that I wasn't completely satisfied in Christ. Was it wrong for me to want this so badly? Afterall, I had been healed from cancer. Wasn't that enough? And more than that, why would God give me the desire for a child if I weren't able to fulfill that? I love how Debra Bidwell explains her longing for a child in her book *The Ache for a Child*:

> "God had the desire to create new life, and He wanted to create it in His own image. If He, being perfect and complete had this desire to create, how could it be selfish or wrong? And because He created us in His image, with many of His attributes, it should come as no surprise that we share His desire to create.
>
> If we yearn to take part in the miracle of creating a new life "in our image" with attributes like our own, and want the intimacy of nurturing our child to maturity, that is only natural. This yearning is God- given and a part of how we are

created. It's no wonder that we feel jarred and confused when we are unable to fulfill it."

Studying scripture and reading books like these made me realize that the desire to see something created in my image, to bear forth a child wasn't wrong. It was God-given. Jesus even did that! We share his desire to create. As I allowed God to reveal truths to me like these, I began to let go of my plan and lean into His.

Realizing That Ignorance is Just That

When I was just ten years old, I lost my dad in a car accident. It was obviously an extremely hard time for my entire family. It was a time where we grieved hard, loved hard, and trusted God to carry us, and He did. I remember even then, as a ten-year-old girl hearing people say the craziest things. My mom would handle it graciously when people would say things like, "Well at least he didn't suffer," or "Whose fault was the accident?" But I quickly learned that these people were well meaning, but they were just ignorant.

I think often times the word "ignorant" gets a bad reputation, but there are things I am ignorant about. I rarely know what the weather is going to be. I really don't care to tell you the truth. And it bites me in the butt on a regular basis when I walk outside with a sweater to learn it is going to be 70 degrees that day! But, I remain ignorant in that area. Maybe I need some prayer- pray for me please☺!

But people are ignorant with death. People are ignorant with cancer. And people are ignorant when it comes to infertility. Their perspective is completely innocent, and because I kept that in perspective during both cancer and infertility, it rarely affected me negatively, because I realized what it was- innocent ignorance.

When people would tell me of their aunt, mother, or friend who recently died of breast cancer, I know their intent was good and they were trying to connect with me, even though when I heard things like that and fear tried its hardest to grab a hold of me.

And it didn't also did not help when people tried to push parenthood on us, or when people tried to give us "ideas" on how to start a family!

Yes, I know most people have good intentions, but the advice of sexual techniques, "don't stress", "just relax" from most people didn't necessarily always sit well with me. And if you know me, you know I have over-researched on everything! Including ways to make a baby. Yes, I'm sure someone will say that's the reason I'm not pregnant- because I've researched too much☺. But, for someone trying to have a baby, this kind of advice can be alcohol in a wound. Because infertility, barrenness, childlessness hurts. When you hope for something with all you are and many people give advice on how to make something happen, and it doesn't, you can feel worthless and purposeless. Yes, these are lies of the enemy, but I am just being honest with what it feels like.

Even when people would say that I just needed to wait until I got pregnant on our own instead of pursuing adoption, or that we didn't need to do IVF, or told me a story of someone who adopted a child with lots of problems—I really trust that they were doing it out of a good place, but even if they weren't, I still had to respond correctly. I would note that if I prayed for that person, it would not only bless me, but make me have compassion and forgiveness for them. Colossians 4:6 (NIV) says:

"Let your conversation be always full of grace, seasoned with salt so that you may know how to answer everyone."

I always strove to respond with grace. One of the things I also realized is that most people just don't know how to respond to suffering. Even with all my training as a therapist, there are still situations that come up that leave me speechless. But when I learned how to forgive people's ignorance and see their hearts, it allowed me to see them in a different light and put me at a better, more peaceful place. And peace was something I was striving for with all of me!

One of my dear friends, Christi, was incredibly good at being sensitive to me. Any time we would talk about baby stuff, she would mention that she knew it was hard for me. This same friend contacted me when she found out she was pregnant and personally talked with me before she announced it because she knew it would be difficult for me. That meant the world. I had another close friend do the exact same thing. My friend, Erin, said she had been dreading telling me she was pregnant because we had been wanting a baby for such a long time. Was I not going to be happy for her? Of course I would be happy for her! It was just simply the acknowledgement that meant the world.

My mother-in-law was fantastic at having compassion on us as well and voicing that compassion. She would always bring it up and acknowledge that we were hurting. We had the world's best friends contact us after baby dedications, mother's days, father's day, etc..., and just tell us that they loved us and were praying for us. That meant the world. And that made those people that were a little more ignorant easier to take. Seeing how people loved us through this and acknowledged our pain made the difference for us in being hopeful instead of completely hopeless countless times.

Fertility, Miscarriage, and Stillbirth Jealousy

It is hard for me to even write the title of this section. I erased and re-wrote it several times, because it is just horrible to admit and write down. But, I have been painfully honest thus far, and I commit to continue to do so. I know it is risky in writing from the deepest parts of me, but I am sure this is what God wants me to do.

As many can relate, the infertility journey is not easy on many levels. But, when you are twenty-something and seemingly everyone around you is pregnant and having babies, you are eye-to-eye with it day in and day out.

On top of that, if you are involved in church, the attention and magnifying glass put on children, mother's day, baby dedication, parenting classes, etc...are always staring at you in the face. And as I explained earlier, if children were a blessing from the Lord, then what do I have? Infertility is certainly not a blessing. I guess it can turn into one, but it, in and of itself, is not a blessing. But, yes, it's true I struggled with other people who were pregnant, breastfeeding, and even those who had miscarriages and stillbirths. Yes, I said it and it is the worst thing ever to say. I was becoming jealous of those who had miscarriages. How twisted had I become? Even though we lost a baby through IVF, it wasn't termed a miscarriage by medical standards, but we had created an embryo and to me, that was a baby! But nevertheless, I had never been told I was pregnant. I had never been told I was a mom, and I began envying those who lost a child, because at least they knew what it was like to know they were carrying one! For even a period of weeks, days, or months, they were a mommy and had a life growing inside of them.

This type of thinking is sick, huh? But it is true. I had to struggle to keep my mind happy for other people-truly genuinely happy. When I was almost completed with my radiation treatments, we got a call from my brother in-law and sister-in-law. They were calling us to tell us they were pregnant. Just a few months after learning of their pregnancy, my sister and her husband announced that they were pregnant. They would be the first grandchildren on both sides of the family.

I would find myself with such mixed emotions. I just kept praying, "Lord, please help me to be genuinely, truly, happy for them."

But there were times I would break down. On the way home from a radiation treatment when we learned of my brother-in-law and sister-in-law's pregnancy, I lost it and bawled in the car on the way home. I told Josh I was okay, but I just needed a minute. I really was truly happy for them. I guess it just put a magnifying glass on our sad situation and our own empty arms.

Then, on our way home from my sister announcing her pregnancy news a few months later, I remember Josh losing it and crying on the way home. I remember him saying, "I'm ready for you to not have to be so happy for *other* people." It is something that is so hard to put into words, because we were genuinely happy for our siblings, but in that same breath, you start picturing yourself childless while your siblings' arms are overflowing with these "blessings" that you just can't seem to have.

We continued to believe and pray, asking God to give us a baby on *our* terms, which is what we believed His terms were as well. I really struggled with what it meant for God to give us our heart's desires. I knew my heart's desire was to be a mommy. I wanted to experience pregnancy and control every part about my pregnancy. After cancer, I became super aware of the things I was putting in my body, and I wanted to make sure our baby was as healthy as possible! So, I just kept believing that God would give us the desires of our heart, which at the time was pregnancy.

The hard part is, we don't always know exactly what God meant when he spoke things that are now verses in the Bible. Yes, God wants to give us the desires of our heart, but if He gave us the desires of our heart all the time, then it wouldn't be necessary for the Holy Spirit to intercede for us in prayer. Romans 8: 26-27 (NLT) says:

> *"And the Holy Spirit helps us in our weakness. For example, we don't know what God wants us to pray for. But the Holy Spirit prays for us with groanings that cannot be expressed in words. And the Father who knows all hearts knows what the Spirit is saying, for the Spirit pleads for us believers in harmony with God's own will."*

Now, I am no theologian, but if this scripture is correct, then there are times where we don't know what to pray for. God knows our hearts and our desires, but He wants us to experience what is best. I believe that our prayers go through the Holy Spirit and that is when He prays what we really need. So, in essence, our prayers really aren't even our own- they are the Holy Spirit's! Wow- is that frustrating and amazing at all the same time!

God cares enough about each detail that our prayers are "filtered", if you will, through the Holy Spirit. I kept praying and praying for a pregnancy. Each month was filled with ovulation test after ovulation test, then a blood ovulation test, then pregnancy test. Then medication. Then seeing a fertility specialists, special blood tests, gynecological exams, vaginal ultrasounds, in-vitro fertilization- all to accomplish what I wanted. Not that I won't have a biological child in my future, but looking back, I was set out on a goal and praying for my desires, not realizing that the Holy Spirit may be changing those desires.

As we kept pursuing pregnancy, we watched my niece and nephew grow from tiny infants into toddlers. My sister- in-law became pregnant again, and we learned of this news shortly after my failed IVF. More friends became pregnant and many were saddened to learn of "surprise" pregnancies. Many of our friends were on their second, third, and even fourth babies! And here we were-childless. But God also began to help me see both sides. While infertility was a trial for us that was used to change our hearts and I saw being a parent as a tremendous blessing, for someone else, pregnancy might be the trial that God would use to change their hearts. Even when I didn't understand, I tried to trust that He did. Isaiah 55:8-9 (NIV) says:

> *"For my thoughts are not your thoughts,*
> *neither are your ways my ways.," declares the*

Lord. "As the heavens are higher than the earth, so are my ways and my thoughts higher than your thoughts."

Sometimes, we receive less than what God would have for us because we beg and beg for us, when if we just waited and surrendered to His plan, it would turn out much better. This was seen in God conceding to the children of Israel (1 Samuel 8:6-22). I realized I could not manipulate this plan by my own will. God might indeed allow it and me never realize the full extent of what He had for me if I would only surrender.

I realized that through my desire to have a child, I focused so much on God answering my exact prayer and finding scripture to back it up, that I left little to no room for God's sovereignty in this situation. Often times I was just telling Him what to say and how to act without giving Him actual room to be who He is. He is God, you know. But there were times I apparently had it "figured out" better. You would think I would know this by now!

Don't Rush Grief

In cancer, and in my case, breast cancer, there is a lot of grief. Grief of losing your hair. Grief of a terrible disease. Grief of losing normalcy. Grief of sickness. Grief of losing your breasts. Grief that comes with multiple surgeries. Grief from being away from home. The list goes on and on. And then there is the grief that comes with infertility.

There is a difference in accepting a diagnosis, being a "victim" to it, and just simply grieving. I knew being a victim was not going to work for me. I rarely try to feel sorry for myself, simply because it does *nothing*. But accepting and grieving? Yes, I believe both are essential and both do not need rushing.

I remember having conversations early on with people telling me I needed to "accept" my diagnosis. I had a hard time doing this. One day I don't have cancer, and the next day I do? I don't know how anyone can just "accept" something that quickly. For me, and I believe most, it is a process, and that is okay. For true, long-lasting, healthy acceptance, I believe it takes time. It can't be rushed.

For grief, I believe it takes even more time. You may have read many books on grief. On the stages of grief. For some, grief takes a typical pattern, but for others, it is anything but typical. For me, I would think that I was done "grieving" or moved past a place of fear, then I would hear of someone else whose cancer came back or another young person diagnosed, and fear and grief would jump on me faster than I would have ever imagined. Does that mean I haven't grieved or that I am not "over it"? No, it just means that I am human and that grief takes time. And real, true grief, where there is a deep, painful loss is always there. It may not preoccupy your mind as much as time progresses, but it is always there, and that is okay. It doesn't mean you aren't "over it."

Grief also does not mean you do not have faith. Grief does not mean you don't have hope. Grief doesn't mean you aren't "strong". It simply means that you are human, and it isn't until we mourn that we can truly be comforted. Matthew 5:4 (NKJV) says:

"Blessed are those who mourn, for they shall be comforted."

If this verse is true, which I believe it is, grief gives us the opportunity to be comforted. And I don't know about you, but I could use some comfort in my life. Some real, true, comfort, after my life has been anything but comfortable these last few years. But it won't come in my life or yours until we mourn. Until we grieve. So, here I am still grieving, still living life, but I am comforted because of Jesus. I pray the same for you. Allow yourself to grieve. And give yourself time.

Seeing Infertility as a Gift

Infertility can be a gift. Yes, I just wrote that. Even as I write that, I don't know if I fully believe it. But, hey, sometimes we have to do something or say something before we truly believe it, right? Here I am walking in faith! But it is true.

We are all quick to say that God gives only good gifts. But when it comes to diseases like cancer, or other devastating diagnoses, such as infertility, we see it as a punishment or something so terrible, and it is. Please don't hear me wrong here. But I think that is when I finally accepted my cancer diagnosis and my "infertility" diagnosis- not meaning I couldn't fight it. Not meaning it defined me. Not meaning that I was giving into statistics, but when I finally accepted that this was my challenge at the current moment- this was my reality, I realized that God loved me and that He had bigger plans than I could have imagined. That maybe these terrible, horrible, miserable things in my life were really gifts. Infertility is a gift because through it, we are having our firstborn child. And through cancer, infertility surfaced. So, they were gifts. Yes, they really were. Okay, moving on to the next point because if I read that again, I will erase it. Hard to say they were gifts. But this child is worth it all.

Chapter 9

We Aren't
Starting a Family

After our failed IVF attempt, we didn't know where to turn. What to do. When to do it. We knew we wanted to start our family- there was no doubt in that. But God gave me a revelation one day that we weren't *starting* a family. We already were one. I wrote a blog post to explain my thoughts:

Blog Excerpt
October 11, 2014
We Aren't Starting A Family

> *Yes, you read that right, we aren't starting our family. In fact, we have been a family for over eight years now. Yep, the Taylor family started on July 22, 2006. We are growing our family, but definitely not starting it.*

This is something that God has spoken to my heart lately about. Josh and I are a family and have been way before kids.

Almost a year ago, Josh and I attended an auction where we won a family photo session. We weren't even trying to win the photo session. Josh was just trying to start the bid! So, we laughed when we won it and were honored to buy the item, as the money was going to raise awareness for human trafficking.

So, when we won this photo shoot, we decided to save it and we could use it for a maternity photos. So, we have held onto it for about a year. I've been so excited to use it, but we just kept waiting. Well, you know the rest of the story. We haven't gotten pregnant, thus we still hadn't used our photo shoot.

Photo shoots are for families, right? Or for seniors. Or for newborns, or engagement photos, wedding photos, you get the picture... Well after we learned of our failed IVF cycle, I felt like we should take these photos. God clearly spoke to me: "You are a family."

My brother-in-law and sister-in-law are incredibly photogenic. They have always giving photo books or photo calendars as Christmas gifts as they had their engagement photos, wedding photos, photos of their daughter...year after year they have had certain events in their life that have called for photos!

Josh and I have always laughed and thought, "Well, we could just give pictures of us sitting at our house!" Our life and family didn't seem as "legitimate" or "picture perfect."

Well, we scheduled the photo session. Nope. It wasn't a maternity session, an anniversary session, or a husband, wife, 2 kids and a dog perfect-type session! It was a really fun experience, especially because we never took engagement photos, so it was cool to do that:) But here is what I learned:

Whether you are a single mom, a newly married couple, a young single, an older single, a teenager, a widow or widower, a divorced dad, a grandparent, or a couple that has been married for a while without children—

Josh and Aly Taylor (and Bella) are a family.

We celebrate a "Family Night" at our church one Sunday night of the month. We are asked to set aside special time with our family that night where we do something intentional to spend quality time together .

We often see pictures of families playing games and activities and many times, I am thinking, "It's just us!" But "just us" is an incredibly good thing. We have been able to spend such quality and alone time together and start our family long before we began growing our family. Oh how blessed we are!

We started our family on July 22, 2006. It doesn't happen when a baby enters in.

You started your family when you were born. Or when you had your child.

Or when you got married.

Or when you got divorced.

Or when you were adopted into another family. Or when you created a close friendship.

Lesson of the day: Embrace where you are.

122

Embrace your family. It's already started...don't wait to take your pictures for the "family moment". That moment is today. Do it now. Embrace and enjoy today! Enjoy some of our family photos!

Aly

We started our family the day we took our wedding vows. Yes, we have been trying to grow our family over the last three and a half years, but we already were a family. I had to keep that in the forefront of my mind when we were striving to grow our family. We weren't incomplete. In Jesus we were complete, and in each other, we found whom our souls loved.

It was during this time, after failed pregnancy attempts, that we did some major soul searching on what to do next. We knew God wanted us to be parents, but the plethora of parenting options were often more overwhelming than exciting. We knew we were already a family, and it was during this time of seeking God's hand that he revealed much to me about what we already were.

We were a family. We didn't *need* a baby to show God's faithfulness. Or even that he holds true to his promises.

Hadn't he already done enough? Miraculously healed me of cancer? Healed my husband of pride and transformed him? Healed relationships through the process? A promise of a baby was not riding on His goodness. He was good- baby or not. We had to put that in the forefront as we sought out other options. We weren't starting our family- we were growing it.

Adoption?

I remember God speaking to my heart about adoption before I was fully allowing Him to. Ha, yes, I guess he can do that. He is God, you know? He would nudge my heart when I heard an adoption story. He would also really speak to me when someone would approach me about adoption and tell me the story of their children or how they came to adopt. During that time, I was so "me" focused, on "me" getting pregnant, on "me" having a baby—seeing the miracle of God restoring my womb.

Once we had our failed IVF cycle, we spoke at length of what we were going to do next. Our options were: continue trying on our own, try IVF again, consider egg donation, or adoption.

When we went for our follow-up appointment with my fertility doctor after our failed IVF, he basically said that we would have the slimmest to no chance of getting pregnant on our own. He strongly pushed going through with an egg donation. I had every ability to carry a child-it was just creating one that was the issue.

Wow, we left that day with so many options and not a clue of what to do. I remember saying "I'm so sorry," so many times on the way home and Josh hating for me to say that. His general response was, "We have no idea that it wasn't me!" But, since his sperm count looked perfect, and my quality and quantity of eggs were low, it didn't take me long to rule that statement out! We discussed everything possible under the sun on the way home. Would it be weird for me to carry another woman's baby through egg donation? Could we even go through IVF again? If we did adoption, where do we even start?!

Here we were confused again. Not only about why I didn't get pregnant, but even more confused about the direction to move toward. This wasn't a decision about buying a car, where you weigh the options and decide. This was a baby! The gravity of that decision and that weight was and is HUGE!

God's Plan Begins to Unfold

Shortly after we told our parents that we weren't pregnant, my mom approached me with a possible adoption situation. A little boy was going to be born soon and there was a possibility that the mother was going to put him up for adoption. My mom just basically checked in with us and asked our thoughts. I was taken aback at first and thought I would discuss it with Josh. I explained the situation and asked what he thought, and he immediately said, "Yes, we're interested. What do we need to do?"

After the initial shock of him not even taking a second to think, I realized that this was it. I know that sounds very anti-climatic, but that was it for me. It was in that moment, that I knew that adoption was the next step for us. I knew I was open and ready for it, but I guess because I thought the fertility issues were "my fault," I needed to make sure my husband was ready to move forward with the next step. That was all I needed right there. God revealed to me that it had been in my heart all along. I just needed to know that Josh was in agreement, and more importantly that this was God- led and not "us"- led.

I've always loved Josh's heart for orphans. For anyone needy, for that matter. I always knew that if we went on a mission trip and saw different orphanages, that we would be coming home with lots of babies. I love his compassionate heart and his willingness to help, serve, and love on those who need to be loved. He has always wanted to adopt, but we thought the timing would be different! Oh, how His timing is always better!

We continued to feel confirmation for moving forward with adoption. I wanted to move slowly. Yes, we wanted children years ago, but I know that haste makes mistakes. And this was our child we were talking about! I wanted to make sure we were walking in God's will and not moving by our own accord or only our selfish desires. One particular conversation sticks out to me when we felt God leading us toward adoption and I was seeking his will on the situation. Here is a conversation at lunch with my friend, Lauren, where my eyes became opened:

I meet my friend, Lauren for lunch and we always love getting together. She is one of my best friends. We met in graduate school and went on to get our PhD's together. I literally don't know what I would do without her. Therapists make the best friends, because we listen and typically can give each other sound advice. It's much easier giving someone else advice than taking our own!

Anyway, this particular day I am really struggling. Struggling discerning God's will and asking Him for guidance and wisdom concerning our adoption journey. I explain to Lauren that adoption is scary. How do I know if this is right for us? We are praying and asking God to lead us and here we are, but will I mess up His plan if we move forward on this? What if I move too soon? What if I move too fast? Lauren looks at me and says, "How could taking care of an orphan not be God's will, regardless of the timing" Tears. We both are in tears. She was so right.

God's word talks about taking care of the widows and orphans, so I don't even have to question God's will. She goes on to tell me that if we are seeking God and obeying Him, He is sovereign. As long as we are walking and trusting His sovereignty, He will guide and lead us. She explains for me to rest in that.

The exact same advice I may have given to someone else, I needed myself. It was this day, this lunch, where I know beyond a shadow of a doubt that we were in the middle of God's will, and I had to stop questioning it all. If I believed that God was sovereign, I was really questioning God, and that had to stop. I had to rest in who God was and trust that He is sovereign over all.

Don't Go to War Without Advice!

Once we felt God leading us to adoption, I knew that we needed help. Not only literal help, because this adoption world and adoption-talk was so foreign to us, but I needed people's wisdom, advice, and direction as we were about to go down that path.

For several months before we officially applied for adoption and began making official steps down that road, I called literally every person I knew who had gone through a domestic adoption. I asked questions. We cried together and prayed together. But here's the amazing thing- with every conversation there was more confirmation that this was *always* the plan.

Honestly, I felt stupid for not realizing this sooner. Why did we go through IVF and spend all that money when we could have done this from the beginning? But God knew what we needed. He knew we needed to go through that to get to this place.

I became part of another sisterhood. When I was diagnosed with breast cancer, I remember one woman telling me that I was now a part of a club that no one ever wants to be a part of- a breast cancer sisterhood. And, boy, is that so true! We can talk on a level like no others can understand. I imagine it's the same for parents of special needs children, or someone who has lost a child or spouse--- there is just a level of instant connection there that cannot be made with human effort.

So, now I was a part of two other clubs. The infertility club and the adoption club. I want to say I wish I weren't a part of the cancer club. I want to say I wish I weren't a part of the infertility club. But, if I weren't a part of those clubs, I don't know if I would have ever met my babies, and because of that, I am grateful for these clubs. And the adoption club is the best club in the world to be a part of. How exciting to be a part of a group that welcomes children into their lives and families to be loved and adored, forever. I love the adoption club.

But it is true, the cancer club and the infertility club aided in making me a part of the adoption club, which helped me become a mommy. Amazing to see how cancer, yes, cancer, made me a mommy. And boy did I need advice on adoption and motherhood! Here is a blog post I wrote on the essentialism of wisdom and advice:

Blog Excerpt
November 23, 2014

When we felt God leading us to adoption, we were clueless. How does it work? Are we going to adopt internationally or domestically? Do we go through an agency? An attorney? Do we just pray for someone to come to us that is not ready to be a mother?

Needless to say, we had lots of questions and were unsure about much if not all of it. It was SO overwhelming! As I mentioned in an earlier post, God has always put a heart for adoption in us, but we were just unsure of the timing.

"For by wise guidance you can wage your war, and in abundance of counselors there is victory." Proverbs 24:6

This verse above in Proverbs talks about victory. We have experienced God's victory in so many areas of our life- victory over cancer, paralyzing fear, spiritual and emotional healing of my husband, but we don't stop there. We want victory in every area of our life- including our growing family with this adoption process!

It has almost been six months since we learned I wasn't pregnant and since that happened, I have continually heard God telling me to not rush into anything. When you have wanted a family for so long, it is really easy to make a hasty decision to just grow our family- whether that be IVF again, a quick adoption agency application- or whatever. But I have tried to move slowly...And we are feeling peace to apply to an agency/attorney in January.

Another thing I have continued to heed God's advice on is to get advice! Over the past several months, I have attempted to contact as many people as possible who have gone through a domestic adoption. Wow- have I gleaned so much from their advice!

They have prayed for me, cried with me, answered a million and one questions from me, given me connections and shared their amazing experience of growing their own families.

Adoption is a hard road. And the most rewarding at that. To understand what we are doing- what this means for our future baby and for us- it has connected me to God's heart like nothing ever before.

How he CHOSE us and ADOPTED us as his own...wow, I get teared up just writing that down.

And if I already feel that way without having our miracle baby in our arms– I literally CANNOT imagine how we will see God in every step of this adoption process.

But asking for all this advice and seeking others experiences, opinions, and emotional and

*physical wisdom- it has made me ponder, why
don't I do this in other areas of my life? Sure, I do
it in some. But often times I make decisions on my
own. I am pretty independent. And I even pray
about it. God's opinion is most important, right?*

*Yes, that is right. But if I believe that, then I
have to do what he says on getting advice from
others before making crucial decisions.*

*These are the questions I've been
contemplating:*

*Why don't I seek always seek advice before I
make a crucial decision?*

*Before I bring up something difficult to
Josh? Or to a family member?*

Before I take a job? Or don't take a job?

*Why don't I always seek advice on how to
handle a tense situation?*

*The funny thing is, we DO ask advice on so
many things in life.*

*Typically it's the smaller things—From
clothes, to colleges, to baby items– I see it on
social media all the time. "Moms, what are the*

good car seats?" And, I'm sure I will be asking questions like these very soon:)

And the even more ironic, funnier thing is that I give advice all day, every day for a living. And oh how I respect those who seek advice. What that says about their character and obeying God! May I do the same.

"Where there is no guidance, a people falls, but in an abundance of counselors there is safety." Proverbs 11:14

But I have gleaned so much emotional support and advice from these amazing families. How much better equipped I am for this journey having sat down for lunch, or coffee, or hour long phone calls!

I encourage you to seek advice for whatever it is you are going through. Maybe it's a parenting issue. Or a friend issue. Or something at work. Or taking a job. Going back to school. Something in your marriage. Advice on a relationship— the list is endless.

We all need advice in one way or another. We just have to be vulnerable enough to share what it is we need help with.

Whether it be a counselor. Or a trusted friend. Or a parent. Or your spouse. DO IT! My future children will be grateful for me taking so much time seeking advice about adoption. And I can guarantee you and yours will be better because of it. AND, when you do it, you are obeying God's word- that is enough reason in and of itself!

Love you guys,

Aly

Chapter 10

Adoption: The First and Best Choice, All Along

It is amazing to look back and see that adoption was the first, best choice all along. This was never a "second choice" or a "back-up" plan. Looking back, we just see that we had to go through what we went through to get to this place. I hate hindsight. I wish foresight was much more telling! But hindsight is truly 20/20 and God is all-knowing. It baffles me that I just don't rest in Him and His plan more often.

As someone who has dreamed of motherhood and pregnancy my whole life, I wondered what this adoption process would be like. I knew other adoptive mothers said that it was just as much of a connection process as pregnancy, but honestly, I didn't know if they were really telling the truth! I mean how can having someone else's (biological) baby be the same as having your own? Well, I am here to tell you, IT CAN! God began changing our hearts as soon as we followed His call to adoption. I shared some of this transformation in a blog post:

Blog Excerpt

December 18, 2014

What Makes A Mother?

Josh has always talked about adoption. For me, it was something that I had to wrap my mind around. As a mom, I always dreamed about feeling a little one inside of me. It really is crazy. I've heard pregnant moms talk about this all the time. How much they already love the little life growing inside of them. When you feel that little human inside of you and actually experience the miracle that is creating another life, there is a bond that forms even before that baby is born.

I've counseled couples going through pregnancy and done TONS of research on pregnancy. I laugh at the search history on my computer-- everything you could possibly see about trying to get pregnant- I mean EVERYTHING!:) Often times a mother experiences more bonding and love with the baby during the pregnancy than the father.

Typically, this is quite simply because she is the one carrying the baby. You often times see pregnant moms rubbing or holding their bellies. Yes, I've heard often time they itch and it feels good to hold their belly, but it also is an innate love and affection for that child growing!

Sometimes fathers can seem removed from the process as their wife is experiencing so many physical changes while they are just looking on and not necessarily experiencing the same things. The same can be true with breast feeding, as moms are the ones providing for the children in a way that the father cannot. It can be an incredibly special time for moms and a hard time for dads to find their connection to the baby.

I have always looked forward to pregnancy. I've heard many moms say, "If I just didn't have to go through a pregnancy again, I would have more." Often times this is said by a mother who had extremely hard pregnancies, or someone who was very sick. And I can so understand that.

But then there are some who just simply don't like being pregnant. Don't like gaining weight. Don't like the birthing process or breast-feeding. And that is totally okay.

That just isn't me. Maybe it would be me if I experienced a terrible pregnancy, but I've always looked forward to pregnancy.

I couldn't wait to get pregnant. Seriously, my whole life. I couldn't wait to grow and wear maternity clothes. I couldn't wait to feel and experience a miracle inside of me. I've always wanted to experience natural childbirth. I know many moms will think I'm crazy here, but I just have. I have a pretty high pain tolerance and would like to experience what the natural birthing process is like. I even have a good friend that has said that she would be my mid-wife. I mean, I had the whole thing planned out:)

The idea of breast-feeding is amazing. Just to even really think about how God created our bodies to provide everything our babies would need- amazing. Now, I know there are many moms out there, just like me who wanted everything naturally, who wanted to breast feed, all to find out she couldn't have a natural delivery or breast feed. So, you ladies out there can relate with me.

Honestly, one of the hardest parts about my mastectomy surgery was losing the ability to breast-feed. I really think I was more upset about that than the cosmetic outcome. I have just always wanted to experience it and to obviously give my child the nutrition that comes from breast-feeding.

DISCLAIMER Now, this is not a sap story of all the things I wish I could have had. I am just first being honest with you guys on how I have had to grieve the above things. Please hear my heart as you read this and please don't judge me on sharing with you guys!

But here's the bottom line. Most of the things I listed above are selfish. Are they God-given desires? Yes. Do I believe God created me to be able to experience these amazing things that only women are physically able to do? Yes. Do I realize that it is okay for me to desire these things? Yes! But have I realized that most of these "pregnancy" things are for my benefit? A loud, Yes!

Wow, that was a pill to swallow. To realize that when I focus on all of those things, it becomes "me" focused. Not focused on our baby. My pregnancy. My birth plan.

My breastfeeding. I hate that at the current time I'm not able to birth a baby. But I am praying for the incredible birth experience that will occur with our child and his/her birth mother.

I hate that I won't be able to breast feed, but it will allow both Josh and I to be able to bond with the baby and hopefully get some more help (and sleep:)), as all of the feedings won't revolve around me. I am praying that we find the most natural way to feed our baby to give him/her the nutrition they need. God will provide and protect.

I hate that I won't be in a hospital room for all our friends and family to come and visit and ask about the birthing process etc...But what do these things have to do with our baby? Not much at all. It's mostly about me. About Josh and me.

It has to do with me doing all the "mother" things. But that isn't what makes me a mother- **love does.** *And yes, there are still moments where I*

144

yearn to feel a baby growing inside of me, but it is amazing what God has done in our hearts and lives once he opened our hearts to adoption. The excitement I had for pregnancy has been times 100 thinking about adoption. I can honestly say this adoption process has been more exciting than I could imagine of a pregnancy. In many ways, I think it is better.

So, as you just read, my whole definition of what a mother is and was began changing. It was less about me. More about God's baby and His plans for our family. It can sound good to say, "We just want God's plan," but when you totally surrender and when God forces you to totally surrender (unsuccessful pregnancy attempts, no pregnancies with fertility medication, failed IVF), it becomes abundantly clear what His plan is. Adoption was it from the beginning. The peace that came over me once I learned this piece of our story and that this was my path to the dream He put in my heart as a little girl- it literally was better than any pregnancy that I could imagine.

Here below, I finish up the previous blog post by explaining some of my emotions while thinking of mothers and specifically our future birth mother:

Blog Excerpt from above

> *Mothers are some of the most unselfish people I know. I remember talking to one of my good friends after she became a mom, and she said, "I just can't believe how selfish I was before I had kids! I don't even remember what I did with all that free time!"*
>
> *Moms (and dads) are always taking care of their little ones and putting their needs first.*
>
> *This adoption process has given me an opportunity to realize that adoption is such a beautiful portrayal of a mother's love. A birth mother placing her child in another mother's hands to love and care for- selfless. An adoptive mother willingly raising and loving a child she did not birth- selfless. Both mothers making a choice that will change their lives and their baby(ies) life in every way. It's about the baby. Not me. Not Josh. Not my desire to experience all the things*

146

that come along with pregnancy. It's like someone who focuses so much on the wedding and not the marriage. Well, because of our adoption, it has us so focused on our baby. Not my pregnancy. Not a birth plan. Not breast feeding or parenting books. Just our baby. Our miracle. The child(ren) that God knew was ours from the time we were created. We just can't get over how much we love this baby and to see those selfish desires go away and be totally focused on our baby and his/her birth mom----that is incredible.

I just keep thinking about what an incredible mother our birth mom is (even when we don't know who she is). After all, our own Savior gave His only son to us all—what a selfless God, what a selfless birth mom we have, what a transformation God has done in our hearts...

MERRY CHRISTMAS!!! Celebrate with us as we celebrate the birth of the one who adopted us into his family forever. I love adoption. I love it even more because it all started with Christ.

Loving this transformation God is doing in us,

Aly

This has to be AT LEAST as incredible as pregnancy, if not more....

Adoption> Pregnancy

Adoption began to become much more exciting to me than pregnancy ever could, and I never thought I would be able to say that honestly. Whereas I used to see a pregnant woman and be sad, I now thought of our birth mom. While I used to go to baby showers and wonder if that would ever be me, I knew it would be. Pregnancy was a possibility while adoption was a path to becoming a mother, no question about it. There were so many children out in the world that desperately needed a Christian family! How exciting is it that that I get to do that!?! What a privilege. What an honor.

Now, please hear my heart here. I, of course, believe that pregnancy is amazing, and it is a miracle of God. There still is a slim chance that I could get pregnant at some point, and if that is God's plan for us- bring it on! I am not saying that adoption is actually better than pregnancy. I am just trying to convey how God changed our hearts about it all.

I no longer *craved* pregnancy. I no longer was taking ovulation tests and pregnancy tests each month (or each week☺). For the first time in years, I actually was hoping I *wasn't* pregnant. Did I just type that? Yes that's the truth. I felt so strongly about adoption that pregnancy was no longer even that appealing. So, if that doesn't give you a piece of the transformation that has occurred in me, I don't know what will.

Chapter 11

Adoption: Where To Even Start?

Once we knew we were in the middle of God's will concerning adoption, there were still lots of practical parts to it. If I typed in the word "adoption" on Google, literally hundreds of agencies, attorneys, and private adoption options would come up! What do I go with? How do I do this?! I know that this is me thinking outside of God's sovereignty, but I would think, "If I choose this option over another, that is an entirely different baby!" Crazy to think about, and it was incredibly overwhelming.

Honestly, I think many people don't adopt because it seems entirely too overwhelming. They see it as expensive, all the risks involved, and they are not sure how it all works, so they surpass it. And yes, even though the process seemed overwhelming, I was ready and willing to take it on. I just didn't have a clue how. That is where it became incredibly important for me to reach out for advice. I could have done all the research in the world, but if I had not reached out to those who had adopted before or knew much on the subject, I would have been so ill-equipped. And, in the process, I gained support, both emotionally and pragmatically.

But still, after talking to over ten different women who shared their adoption stories with me, I was still confused about which avenue to take in order to bring home our baby. We knew at that particular time in our lives that we weren't called to "foster to adopt", but outside of that, we weren't feeling a clear direction on a certain agency, attorney, or adoption consultants. I filled out paperwork for at least three different agencies to just have it all ready for when we did turn our paperwork in and decided on a direction. Because we weren't having incredibly clear direction on whom to adopt through, I kept feeling peace to wait until after Christmas 2014 to submit our paperwork to an agency.

But, if you know me, it was hard for me to just sit on my hands and wait! So I researched and asked questions on what we could do in the meantime while waiting to decide on whom to go through. After speaking to several different resources, we decided to go ahead and work on our home study. This is basically a study on your home and family to make sure that your child would be brought into a safe and loving home. Just looking at this paperwork was intimidating, but I had to be doing something!

The Home Study

Financial statements, employment verification, birth certificates, physicals, detailed questionnaires, reference letters, insurance policies, tax records, and the list goes on and on! We had to fill out all of this paperwork and get all the required documents, which took a little while to get, but it did make us get more organized! Hey, I had to find something positive out of it!

We were incredibly blessed because one of our friends gave us a name of a social worker who did independent home studies, and we were able to get it done fairly quickly. Along with all the paperwork, a home study in Louisiana requires two at-home visits where your home is inspected with in-depth interviews of the couple both individually and together.

When we decided to have our home study, I wasn't sure what to think or how to prepare for it. The one thing I kept picturing was from the movie, "What to Expect When You're Expecting," and Jennifer Lopez is freaking out when the social worker arrives, hiding pictures and is extremely anxious.

But other than that picture in my head, that is all I knew of a home study. So, before our home study, I was panicking. Josh was making fun of me, as I was cleaning the apartment and our closets from top to bottom! I read every blog about home studies and articles I could find that would help us appear like good parents! Here is a picture into one of our home study visits:

"Okay, at first I like to talk to the parents together and then I will talk to the mom and dad individually." As these words come out of our home study social worker's mouth I can hardly believe she is talking about us. For the first time, we were referred to as parents. Josh was referred to as "dad" and I was referred to as "mom." I am holding back tears at just the beginning of our meeting!

Out of my nervousness, I notice a book labeled "Divorce Care" in our living room. It is for a divorce support group I plan to counsel for therapy, but out of my self-consciousness that day, I say, "I just wanted to let you know that I am a therapist and I am leading a divorce support group. We don't have plans to divorce." She looks at me and laughs, as I can tell she knows I am just talking out of my head. Did I really just say that?! I am now just telling myself, "Shut up, Aly, shut up!"

I know some of you adoptive moms out there have gone through this home study process before and can so relate with me, but I just acted like a crazy person. You just want to appear so capable! I could tell funny story after funny story about those visits. Josh making jokes about us being drug dealers and me cringing with every part of my being, cleaning our apartment from top to bottom, me eavesdropping on Josh's "private" interview and laughing at his answers.

For the record, I wasn't necessarily intentionally eavesdropping, but when you have a one-bedroom apartment, me going into our bedroom didn't necessarily cut out all the noise. As I heard him answering questions on our marriage and his family of origin, she gets to the question of how he expects things to change once a baby arrives. He naively says, "Not too much. We plan to take him/her with us wherever we go." I'm assuming he was saying this half way seriously and halfway joking, to which she replies, "Um, well you'll have sleepless nights, different schedules, more costs..." And Josh says, "Oh, yeah." That's my man!

Honestly though, the home study was not nearly as intimidating as I thought it would be. Our social worker could not have been any more wonderful. She was able to do a "marathon home study", where she did our visits close together, so we could get those done quickly. Yes, we scrubbed the floors and cleaned out our closets, and oddly enough she didn't even look that closely at the cleanliness of our apartment. It was more making sure hazardous things were out of the way of a baby. And the questions were invasive, but I really felt like it was necessary for adoption, and I was thankful to have seen how the process works.

At the time of our home study, we were in a one-bedroom apartment while we were in the middle of building our home. I was extremely nervous about this because I assumed that the baby would need to have a room of his/her own. Thankfully, they only require more than one bedroom when you are adopting a baby over the age of one. Since we were adopting an infant, we were okay to have one bedroom! It's funny the things I stressed over and then when I brought it up to the "powers that be", they acted like it was no issue. After our home study visits were completed, we then waited to be officially "home study approved." It looked like it was all going to work out, as we would likely be approved around Christmas time, and as I said earlier, we were waiting until after Christmas to officially submit our adoption paperwork. So, even though we weren't "actively" seeking adoption because we had not chosen an agency/attorney, I was busy getting everything lined up for when we turned the paperwork in.

Can a Cancer Survivor Adopt?

I still get aggravated at myself at times at why we didn't start out at adoption. I know that God had to lead us there, but we could have bypassed so much hurt and saved a ton of money! But as I look back, I realized one of the main reasons I did not seek out adoption from the beginning. It all came down to me being scared that I would not be allowed to adopt because of the severity of my cancer diagnosis. I don't think I could handle being told I couldn't adopt. Number one, because I so desperately wanted to be a mother and number two, the fear that could abide if I realized that my doctors were deeply concerned about my length of life.

When we started first thinking of adoption, I began looking into really well-known adoption agencies. This was before I talked to friends I knew, and I was just surfing the Internet. The first one I came to, I went to the Frequently Asked Questions page and there it was: "Can I adopt if I am a cancer survivor?" The answer: "Yes and No." Yes, a cancer survivor could adopt, but they had to be at least five years post diagnosis and had to have all medical records and a letter from their oncologist indicating an expected normal life span.

I froze when I read this. Completely froze. Not only was I not yet over five years (almost three) of being cancer- free, but I didn't know if my doctor would be able to provide this documentation that agencies needed! From anything that I accidentally came across (since I strive with all that I am to avoid statistics), my type of cancer has a high likelihood of recurrence, which would indicate a shorter lifespan. I remember turning off my computer abruptly and just telling myself to breathe, praying and trusting God that if this was what we were supposed to do, it would happen.

As I came to find out, the "five year rule" is not as concrete at each agency and attorney. I talked to several agencies and attorneys that said that as long as they had a letter from the oncologist and a substantial amount of time had passed (which qualified me) that it shouldn't be a problem. So, now all I had to wait on was the letter. Here is a glimpse into the process of waiting for and receiving the letter from my oncologist:

I email my oncology nurse, Angela, and explain that we are adopting! I tell her that we need a letter from my oncologist explaining that not only does she recommend us as good candidates for adoption, but speaks well of my health and anticipates a normal life span. I press send as fast as I can. I intentionally do not check my "my MD Anderson account" that day, because I am scared of what it will say. I check it the next day. New message. All it says is that she will forward it to our doctor.

This is typical of our nurse. She is a great nurse, but very short in her email responses. I am trying to not read too much into it, but it is hard to not think, "She didn't say anything about it because she expects our doctor to not be able to write it." So, I wait another day. Angela says she faxed it, as well as placed the letter in the mail. I still have no clue what it says. I check the fax machine. No fax. I check the next day. No fax. I contact Angela again and she says she faxed it, but if I didn't get it, it will come in the mail soon.

Two weeks, yes TWO weeks, pass, and I still haven't gotten the letter! I correspond with Angela again, and she tells me that sometimes mail gets out slow at the office. I mean, seriously? Seriously? This is torture.

After three weeks and no letter, my nurse says my oncologist will need to write another letter, as apparently the other one was lost. Well, my oncologist is out of town! Angela lets me know she found the original letter and is going to fax it again- AHHH! Finally. I see the fax come in and go to Josh's office to read it. I wanted to read it together. I wasn't sure what it would say. Would it say "Aly has a favorable chance of living to 40?" or "Aly has a few more good years." Oh it was so hard to believe.

Josh isn't in his office. I'll wait on him to read it. After a long two minutes, I change my mind. I can't wait. I'm reading it now. I turn over the letter to see the shortest paragraph ever. But it was the best paragraph ever. My doctor said that I had breast cancer, I had the best possible outcome possible and I have a less than 5 % chance of the cancer recurring, therefore an expected average- long life span.

Weeping. Here I am weeping in Josh's office. Praising God once again. I realize right here and now that this information was a big

161

hurdle in me saying "yes" to adoption when the answer was "yes" all along.

Each time Josh and I go for my oncology check-ups, we don't ask too many questions. I imagine most people are asking lots of questions. Many people, especially cancer patients, as I've come to find out, like to hear their "odds" and statistics, and I just don't. I couldn't read websites during my cancer treatment, and I still can't! Maybe one day I can, but as of right now, I just can't.

So needless to say, to know that I had to have a letter from my cancer doctor basically telling adoption agencies that my life span would be "average" was one of the scariest things I've ever done. I was petrified to see that paper. To see statistics. Or to see that they would say "5 to 10" years....those are supposed to be words of hope??? Are you kidding me?!?

It is amazing to know that this adoption not only brings us a baby, but brings me, yet again, more evidence of my divine healing and my doctor's witness to it. I couldn't have been more happy and thankful that day. Crying as I even write this right now!

So, we sent off our letter to our social worker and waited. No longer can cancer keep me from growing my family. With that letter, with those words, there was HOPE!

Chapter 12

The Call That Changed Everything

The timeline for sending in our adoption paperwork ended up moved up a couple of weeks! Josh and I discussed everything, and we felt ready to go ahead and submit our paperwork to an attorney here in Monroe. We finally landed at the adoption route we would use! We thought we would wait one more week to finish filling every last thing out and submit everything. We had been told for this particular attorney to expect to wait 9-12 months for a baby. So, we felt like once we submitted everything, we would still have a while until the baby arrived.

Then everything changed. On December 12, 2014, I received an email. For a few months I had signed up on an attorney in Florida's listserv, which is basically an email list of adoptive parents. This attorney sends out emails on potential situations of birth mothers. He will give a detailed report about the birth mother and father, if he has it, along with who the birth parents are hoping will adopt their child. Once you receive these emails, if there is a case you are interested in, you send in an application with a non- refundable fee, along with pictures, and then the birth parents choose out of those couples. It is a different way of doing adoption, but it is a neat way for the birth parents and the adoptive parents to choose each other.

I had been receiving several emails about potential situations, but none had I felt tempted to apply for, as the birth mother may have been wanting a couple in their 40's, or a couple who had children, or a single mom, etc...

Well, on this day it was different. I received this email, and I just had a feeling about it. There really is no way to describe it. As I scrolled down to view who she was hoping would adopt her baby it read: "A couple in their 30's. Strong Christian Faith. Preference will be given to couples with no children."

Yes, I know that description fits tons of couples, but I just had a feeling about it. I had chills as I was reading the entire email. But I was confused, because we had just landed on turning in our paperwork with an attorney in our town this exact week! And this was an entirely different deal, with an attorney in Florida. I wasn't sure what to do, but I knew I had to tell Josh. Here is a little picture of what our conversation looked like:

I said, "Hey, so I got this email about a potential situation in Florida..." and I explain it all to him. He asks me several questions, wise questions about why I am wanting to apply. Such as, "Is it just that you want a baby soon?" "How much of this do you think is you, and how much do you think is God?" Yes, they were really good questions, but at the time I am just wanting him to be excited with me!

After about 20 minutes of conversation and prayer, he says, "Let's apply." I'm thinking, "That's it? No more questions?" He said, "Yes, let's just apply. She still has to choose us."

I was ecstatic that Josh was on board. I loved that he questioned me hard (well, not at the time), but then was on board. We were so giddy! We were having friends over that night, but agreed to not say anything to not let our emotions get too crazy or get too invested. As I was cleaning the house that afternoon and making dinner for our friends coming over that night, I got a call at 4 o'clock. I could tell from the caller ID that it was a call from an adoption attorney in New Orleans. A friend had given me her name as a potential attorney to use for our adoption, but we had since decided to go with the Monroe attorney. Here is our conversation:

> *"Hello?" She starts it off with some small talk and then says, "Remind me of your adoption budget again?" I explain that we obviously can't do everything, but we are not wanting to put a limit on it. If there is a child that God has planned for us to have as our own and raise, He will come up with the funds. She says, "Okay, well we have a birth mom who is due at the end of January (mind you this is December 12), and here is the kicker- she is pregnant with TWINS! Would you and your husband be interested?" I don't even know what to say. We go from no calls and finally feeling peace*

168

to go with an attorney in town and on the SAME day we get two potential situations from two different attorneys. I try to catch my breath and tell her I will discuss with Josh and call her tomorrow. As I hang up the phone, Josh is looking at me like, "Well, what is it?" I explain to him the situation and he says, "Let's do it!" I wasn't so sure whether to dive in with twins. Exciting? Yes. Scared? Yes. Two calls in one day. Wow, wow, wow.

The next morning, we sent off our application packet for the first situation in Florida. We had no idea how many people would be applying for the case, but we knew we would be updated as application packets came in. We decided to spend the next two days telling our families of the potential situations and listening to their thoughts on the both of them. Both were expensive (as most domestic adoptions are), but especially the twin case. As exciting as it was to think about, were we being crazy? We wanted to make sure we were using wisdom.

Here was our application that we sent off to Florida!

Both my mom and my in-laws were incredibly supportive of us applying for both cases. We talked about the difficulties in each. Whether we would be able to raise the money, raise the children☺, and all the practicalities of each. Most of all they prayed with us and believed in God's plan.

After much prayer and consideration, we applied for the twin case as well. We would find out the following week whether we were chosen for either case.

If we were not chosen for either, we planned to stick to the original plan of putting in our application back home.

God, Please Make This Decision For Us!

I know this is how adoptive parents warned us it would be, but to go from nothing to two possible situations in one day! I just couldn't handle it! Now we had to wait around a week on both situations. Honestly, one of my biggest fears was that both birth mothers would choose us. I know how that sounds, but how would we make that decision?! We would just want to take them all, but that would probably not be the wisest thing to do.

The attorney who we were talking with about the twins said there was a very good chance we would be chosen. The birth mother was just 20 years old and wanted an adoptive couple around our age with no kids. We got word that there had been three applications for this case, and now we just had to wait.

I couldn't sleep. I had to force myself to eat. Here we were waiting again. The thing I prayed for most was of course the birth moms, the babies, and of course God's will. And I was praying that at least one would not

171

choose us. If neither was right, I prayed that neither would choose us, but if God could make this decision for us- oh how wonderful that would be! So, we had one of the longest weeks of our lives. We just had to sit back and wait and see if and when we would hear from them. Here is a look back of when I got the call from the New Orleans attorney about the twins:

I am at my hair cut appointment, and I see my phone ringing. It is from the New Orleans attorney. I am under the dryer, and I can't answer the phone. What if she says the birth mother chose us? What if she said she didn't? Either way, I know I can't answer the phone as badly as every part of me wants to. I know I will be emotional either way, so I choose to wait.

Yes, the hairdresser is one of my dear friends, but I just can't do it. So I wait. I get in the car to call the attorney, and of course, she doesn't answer. Ahhhh!!! She finally calls me back. The first words out of her mouth are, "We are incredibly surprised, but the birth mother chose the family who already had children." She explains that the birth mother changed her mind once she saw a profile of a family with an older son and she realized she wanted that for her babies. The attorney was shocked. She went on to say that nothing was wrong with us, and she was incredibly sorry.

I don't take that as a fluke or surprise. That was a direct answer to my prayer. A closed door.

Even though the birth mother had initially said she preferred a couple with no children, she had an older brother and realized how much she would like for her children to have that. The attorney assured me that nothing was wrong with us and that our baby was still out there.

Yes, I was disappointed, but I just had a peace like this wasn't it for us. I find it no coincidence that everything was looking like she would choose us, just to learn that last minute she had a change of heart and went with the family with children (whom they were thinking was a "for sure" no). God is so amazing. He really was making this decision for us.

We then had to wait another day to hear on the other case. I just kept praying for God's will, and if this was not our baby, for her to not choose us. Friday, December 19th came, and all we knew was that we would be notified Friday by email of whom the birth mom chose. I got an update Friday morning that 22 applicants applied for this single case. Yes, you read that right- 22! We had not been chosen out of three, so it was hard to imagine that we would be chosen out of 22. So I checked my email all day long. We had a 33% chance with the twins and now we had a 4% chance of the birth mom choosing us. Yes, we had beaten statistics before with cancer, but we knew that are chances were slim in this case.

I was praying for this birth mom all day, and she was on my mind constantly. I wasn't praying she would choose us. I was praying she would choose the parents for this baby. Then, we got the call that would forever change our lives. Here is some insight into that moment and that call:

I am driving home from picking up food for our Taylor Christmas that night, and I notice a phone call from a Florida number. At first, it catches me off guard because I wasn't expecting a phone call. I was expecting an email. I know that our attorney is located in Florida. Could this really be happening? I'm not sure what to expect. I answer the phone, "Hello?" The man on the other line says, "Yes, this is [attorney], is this Alyssa Taylor?" "Yes". "Did you apply for the [birth mom] case?" "Yes." At this point, I am shaking and hoping I can keep the car between the lines. The attorney says, "Okay, hold on one minute. I have your husband on the other line." Then, the phone hangs up. Really, I mean, REALLY? I'm crying and shaking now. The entire moment is completely surreal. The longest two minutes of my life, and then the phone rings again from Florida. I can now hear my sweet husband's voice on the other end of the phone. I am just imagining what is going through his mind as he has me and Josh on a conference call and explains to us that the birth mother chose us! She chose US!

Josh and I continue to relive that moment to this day. We will just randomly say to each other, probably once every couple of days, "Can you believe that day that the attorney called us?" It was truly an amazing moment. What is even more amazing is how God made the decision for us! We did not have to choose between cases, but rather He chose for us, which is what we prayed for all along! And to be honest, the "no" on the twins a day before the "yes" of our perfect baby made it that much sweeter. And this all happened on the day we were planning on turning in our paperwork and a large sum of money to another attorney to begin opening our "case." Oh, the amazing things that happen when we allow God to be God and we stop trying to control everything!

One of the Scariest Nights of Our Life

The next day after we learned that our birth mom chose us, we celebrated Christmas with Josh's side of the family. We were beyond elated to share the news with them! We ended up getting Josh's parents a calendar of photos of us for Christmas, (I ordered this several months back) and we decorated the entire month of March with adoption verses and sayings, circling the due date and placing at the top, "We're Matched!" It was an incredible day and moment to share with his family.

This was the calendar with photos we gave my mother-in-law for Christmas. This was how the "March" page was decorated.

I was then able to share with my mom, and it was hard getting to her because this was right in the middle of the Christmas hubbub shopping and we had to tell her soon! So, we told her in the mall and got it on video. Not the way we had envisioned it, but we had to tell her soon, as things were happening quickly. What we didn't realize was that our excitement and joy was about to be followed by one of the scariest nights of our life.

Our attorney explained that the next step was meeting our birth mom and making sure we both felt comfortable moving forward with the adoption. With it being during the holidays, we needed to meet soon, and for us that meant meeting in just two days, hence the reason for having to tell everyone so soon! We were blessed with a flight to Florida for the upcoming Monday and began packing all of our stuff. We were heading to fly out Sunday night and meet with our birth mom and a counselor in the morning.

Saturday night we were getting ready for bed, packing for our trip, and just reveling in our exciting news. I checked my email and saw an email from both the mental health counselor and the attorney on our adoption case. Here is what it read and here was my reaction:

"Haven't been able to get in touch with birth mom. If we cannot reach her tonight, we need

to look at cancelling the meeting on Monday." My heart sinks, and I immediately feel like I am going to throw up. Was she having second thoughts? The attorney hadn't talked to her since the day she chose us. Maybe after she chose us, it became more real to her, and she was backing out. I've heard stories of birth mothers doing this- just stopping answering their phones and disappearing. Could this really be happening so soon? We just told our family today! We've booked plane tickets- I can almost see our baby's face. Is this really happening?!

I could barely sleep all night. Josh had been sick, so I was sleeping on the couch. Each time I would wake up (which was most of the night), I just prayed and prayed for our birth mom. That she was okay. That the baby was okay and that God would speak to her heart. That she would make the right decision- whether it was us, her, or someone else. That God's will be done. I remember holding my head in my hands with my head in between my legs and Josh rubbing my back. We both

179

remained silent Saturday night and Sunday morning as well.

Then, we received hope on later that Sunday morning. We got an email from our attorney saying that he was able to get in touch with the birth mother's aunt, who said that she was still planning on us meeting on Monday and for us to keep our plane tickets. Oh, I could breathe again but was still a little worried since no one had talked to the birth mom herself.

All throughout church that day, so many people were congratulating me- a day I had looked forward to for so long, but a part of me couldn't get too excited because of the night that we had before. Josh's dad preached that Sunday morning and announced our exciting news from the pulpit. We were scared to let him do this, but it was growing our faith for sure, even after the horrendous night we experienced.

Then, I got the best news ever. On our way to Sunday lunch, I saw an email entitled "Birth mom. GOOD NEWS." Oh Praise God! The counselor got in touch with our birth mom, and she apologized as her brother was in the hospital all day Saturday, so she had been out of touch. She wasn't backing out. She still wanted to move forward. I immediately felt a release and knew that it would continue to be "good news."

Wow, but that Saturday night made me experience just for a series of hours what so many parents have experienced through adoption failure.

Some experience it at the beginning of an adoption match. Others go through the process, just to have a mom decide to keep her baby at the hospital. I cannot imagine what this must be like. Trauma cannot come close to describing it. I know several of you reading this book have experience adoption failure, and my heart breaks with and for you. I know people say things here like, "Well that just wasn't your baby," or "God was protecting you," and while that advice may be correct, all I can say is I am so terribly sorry. I can't imagine what you have been through and how you are able to keep going.

I will tell you one thing though that night and other scary parts of this adoption process along the way has made me trust in God like never before. I can't control ANY of this. What goes into the birth mother's mouth-whether it be bad foods, drugs, malnutrition. I can't control the situation- whether she continues to decide to place her baby with us or keep it. I can't control the money. We put up the money in faith and are relinquishing control in wisdom. Everything is out of your control in adoption. But that is one thing that makes it tremendously beautiful because God has to supernaturally do it all, because I can't. One of my adoptive mom friends gave us some of the best advice when we had that horrendous night. She said, "You have to place your trust in God, NOT the birth mom."

Wow, did that ring so true in me. I realized even in those last few short days of excitement and potential heartbreak, I was putting my trust in the situation. In the attorney. In the birth mom. All of those avenues were set up to disappoint me. I had to start trusting in God, or else these next three months until our baby was due was going to be crazy.

Obviously cancer and adoption are two totally different things. But just as I at times put my trust in doctors, in medicine, in my care other than God, I felt it rising up again in this adoption. I mean, you would have thought I would have learned by now!

My only constant is Jesus. My cancer healer. My comfort. My rock. My doctor. My source to become a mommy. My promise keeper.

Meeting Her

After our attorney told us that we were officially matched, the next step was meeting our birth mom. At first, I was kind of confused by this. I guess I had always envisioned going to the hospital and someone handing us a baby and having little interaction with the birth mom. Not that I didn't want interaction, but that is just how I had heard of adoption stories in the past.

I was quickly learning that was not so in this case. Apparently, once we were chosen, we were able to have as little or as much contact with our birth mom as she and we felt comfortable, but the first step was meeting her! If either of us felt unsettled about moving forward, then we would not proceed with the adoption, but of course, on our end, we could not fathom that. We had multiple conversations that all ended in us not being able to think of a scenario in which we wouldn't move forward with this situation.

We found out she picked us on a Friday, and just two days later, that Sunday, we flew off to Jacksonville to meet her. To think that it would be months, if not years, until we had a baby, to just in two days time, we are flying to meet the woman that is potentially carrying our baby- talk about a roller coaster!

Neither Josh nor I could sleep much on that Sunday night. It was just a surreal thought to know that a woman we didn't even know could be carrying our baby! As we woke up on that Monday morning, we were just trying to find a way to pass the time until 10:45 when we would meet with her. We went to Krispy Kreme for Josh to eat donuts (how could he even eat?!), and we shopped at TJ Maxx to get her a small gift. We then had about 30 minutes to kill. Josh had gone to the car while I finished checking out at TJ Maxx. As I walk out to the car, this is what I find:

Josh is standing outside of the car. Has someone hit our rental car? Is he okay? He literally is in a blank stare. I walk up to him and the car with my bags of things. He lets me walk right past him, and I put everything in the car. I go to get in the passenger seat and I say, "You coming?" He gets frustrated at me and asks why I am in a hurry. I explain to him that we can grab a couple extra Christmas gifts before our meeting, and he says, "I can't do anything right now." I've never seen him this nervous. So, what do we do for the next 20 minutes? Drive around the parking lot of Panera Bread. Yep, we drive down every aisle. Back and forth. Back and forth again. In complete silence. We know that our birth mom is inside meeting with the mental health counselor about to meet with us. I guess Josh wasn't that crazy not being able to really think about Christmas presents at the moment.

After we got done driving the parking lot, I received a text letting us know we could come inside. Thoughts are going through my head like, "Do I hug her?" "How will I know it is her?" "Will she be obviously pregnant?" "Oh, gosh, what do I even say?!"

Thankfully, our mental health counselor meets us at the entrance door of Panera Bread and directs us to where our birth mother is. I can roughly see her and another woman, which I later learn is her aunt. I immediately greet them both with a hug, and she hugs me so tight. From the beginning of the meeting there are tears. I ask how she is feeling (totally meaning physically), and she asks, "What do you mean?" Obviously, given her current state, she probably right off the bat thought I was asking how she was doing emotionally.

She answers what I think is a ice breaker question in tears explaining how hard this is. I am thinking, "What a STUPID question, Aly!!!" But honestly the tears are a good start, because that is the beginning of seeing her beautiful heart. She did not want to give her baby up for adoption. She just currently could not provide for her like she would want to. This was not abandonment. This was clear that she wanted to make sure that her baby was given the best life possible.

The connection between our birth mother and us was almost immediate. To come from two completely different ways of life and to sit and talk for two hours- that is ALL God! We answered many questions about our marriage and ourselves. She told me about her three other children and as much as she could about the father.

I had all of my questions written out that I wanted to ask her. One of the questions that was of particular importance to me was asking how involved she wanted us to be in the pregnancy, labor, and delivery. I had been praying specifically that I would be able to see an ultrasound and be as involved as possible in the labor and delivery. When we asked that question, she said, "That is totally up to y'all." I remember that answer blowing me away! I quickly told her that *she* was the priority here. The mental health counselor chimed in and said, "What about the delivery room? What about cutting the cord?" To which she replied, "Yes, they can be in there, and Josh can cut the cord. As long as he stays up here (motioning to her head)." We all laughed, and I was just trying to keep my jaw from hitting the floor in amazement.

I had been specifically praying for us to be a part of the pregnancy as much as possible. Ultrasounds, labor, delivery- I knew the chances were slim from hearing of other adoptions, but I knew I could at least present those requests to God. God cares deeply about the desires of my heart. There were moments I questioned if He really knew my desires of motherhood and actually wanted to meet them as I struggled with and continue to struggle with infertility. But how beautiful that He is allowing me to experience this in a completely different way. It is so exciting.

So, we left the meeting with our birth mom with hugs and tears. She just kept saying, "I love you guys so much. I am ecstatic." I will never forget those words. We all were just incredibly put at ease after meeting one another, because you can only tell so much about someone through paper. She had seen pictures of us, but we had no clue what she even looked like! We left with saying that we would get back in contact with one another when another ultrasound was on the horizon- I mean, was this real life? I was just so in awe of God.

This was me with our birth mom and our baby inside of her the day we met her.

As we were walking back to the car, I knew the next step was to email or call our attorney and say we were ready to move forward. We processed things for a few minutes, cried together, and confirmed with one another that it could not have gone any better. I mean, we just met our baby! This is when the obsession began with our little one. When it became very real.

So I got out my phone to send our attorney an email, and I already had a message from him. Of course my heart started pounding, like it does with every email he sent us. I saw it was a short email. I click on it and it reads:

"They love you." Tears.

After we met our birth mother, and we both felt comfortable moving forward, the baby was unofficially officially ours. We knew that our birth mother could back out at any moment, but she officially chose us, and we officially chose her back. At that point, all we could do was wait. We met her on December 22, exactly three months away from her due date. We had 3 months to prepare and plan, but mostly just wait.

Chapter 13

Learning to Enjoy the Waiting

For Those Still Waiting

You may be reading this book right now thinking, "Well, everything turned out good for her. She had cancer, now she is getting her baby, and she lives happily ever after." You may be thinking, "I wish my life was that easy." Well first of all, that is hard for me to imagine someone saying about my life. But, second of all, I understand that some people have gone through *way* more than I could ever imagine going through. And I hate weighing our "problems" against each other. Each problem is significant, even if one seems "bigger" than another. But regardless, you may be thinking that my story ended in a "happily ever after".

Cancer was a way she got her beautiful baby. What a great story. What a great ending. "And they all lived happily ever after..."

Let me say to you, right now, as I am writing this book, I am writing this in faith. There is still a very high chance that our birth mother decides to keep this baby. We are praying and believing this won't happen, but our ending is not "perfect." And even if we do end up with our miracle baby, we still have other concerns.

We are continuing to trust I'll remain cancer-free. I stuggle with problems with my lymphedema (arm swelling from my mastectomy). We are still wondering and thinking about having more children. We know we want more. If we want our children close in age, we would have to start thinking about adopting again soon. We wonder if we can we do this financially again. What are still unsure of what all God has planned for our family. So, to burst the "happily ever after" bubble, this is our current reality. We are walking in faith in every part of our life and trying to enjoy the journey. Why does life have to be so difficult and why are we surprised? God told us there would be troubles in this life and that's what makes me desire heaven more than ever before. John 16:33 (NIV) says:

> *"I have told you all this so that you may have peace in me. Here on earth you will have*

many trials and sorrows. But take heart, because I have overcome the world."

But, even then, you may still find yourself in a place that is much darker and seemingly much more "hopeless" than our current situation. Maybe you or your husband are medically "sterile", and your marriage is suffering as one or both of you strongly desire biological children. Maybe you have gone through several failed adoptions, and while you greatly desire children or more children, you just don't know if you have the emotional capacity to put yourself, your marriage, or your children at risk like that again. Maybe you have suffered multiple miscarriages and you so badly want to believe that God will give you a baby, but you are wondering if it is worth that risk. Maybe you have experienced the trauma of a stillbirth or lost a baby and you are still grieving each moment. Each second. I literally cannot imagine. Or maybe you or someone you love has been diagnosed with cancer. You are constantly fighting faith and fear and are having trouble finding any hope on what to say, what to do, what to think. You don't know what to do next.

But here is what I do know. God cares. God loves you more than you could ever dare to imagine! God hates to see you hurt. And He so badly wants you to run to Him with your hurt. He cries with you and wishes so badly you could see His plan that will come from all of this. He wants you to trust Him with all you have. That is the only way you will get through this.

So often when I listen to God's voice, I hear Him say, "Trust me." Just the other day I was trying to listen to God, and I really believe he said, "Trust me, little girl."

As I heard God tell me this a few weeks ago in my quiet time, my eyes welled up with tears, as I so long to hear the words "little girl." You see, as I explained earlier, I lost my dad when I was young and I greatly long to have his presence in my life. My dad was someone who was easy to talk to, and he loved it when I would come to him to just talk, even if it was about "10-year-old girl" topics like boys and the spelling bee. And if God is really our heavenly father, how much more He wants us to come to and run to Him, to just talk to Him! He created us. He knows the end of the story is good. We just have to trust Him. And just in looking back on my life in the past three and a half years, once I truly trusted Him, I really began to see His plan, not my own, unfold.

But you have to be willing to let go of your own plan and press into His.

In the mean time, why you are waiting, don't rush your grief. Grieving takes time. But I do know that after grief, after mourning, after surrender, there comes joy. And yes, I am experiencing that joy now in my life, and I know yours is on its way. Psalm 126:6 (NIV) says:

"He who goes out weeping, carrying seed to sow, but will return with songs of joy, carrying sheaves with him."

Joy is coming. Just hang on. I may never understand why God allows us to feel such deep pain. So much hurt. Such devastation. But I do know that I am experiencing a joy that few ever know. And that is because I have felt such hurt. I truly believe that we (those of us who have experienced unimaginable loss) have the chance to experience immense joy that others aren't aware even exists.

Joy. Get ready. It's coming.

The Irony in Our Wait

It's funny that I am such an impatient person. Obviously, none of us are really fond of waiting, but when you think about life, it is all about waiting. Waiting for the day to end, waiting for the summer, waiting for a test grade, waiting for a holiday, waiting for a baby, waiting at Walmart, waiting to have children or grandchildren---everything is about waiting. So why don't we just embrace it, because apparently, life it a lot about waiting!

For us, it has seemed even more prevalent. Waiting for my biopsy results to come back, waiting to get an appointment at MD Anderson, counting down my cancer treatments, waiting the two years to start trying for a family, waiting to get pregnant, waiting and anticipating our IVF results, and then now, waiting on our baby. Yes, that is where we find ourselves today- waiting on HER.

Yes, our baby is a girl! When we learned our baby was a girl, I was ecstatic. It is kind of funny because I've always pictured myself as a mom of boys. I am very laid back, and I always pictured a "little Josh" running around, muddy, and surrounded with sports. But after I was diagnosed, I had several people tell me that they had dreams where we had a little girl. One person said she had a dream we had two girls! I started thinking, "Well, maybe we will have a girl!" So, when we learned I was having a girl, we were both overjoyed.

I also think there was a part of me that was scared of having a little girl, biologically. Being a breast cancer survivor, I knew if I had a little girl, without the constant help of Jesus, I would often worry if she would be predisposed to breast cancer. You are at a higher risk if your mother or aunt had breast cancer, and I think it was always a fear in the back of my mind. So, to get to experience a little girl, without those fears--- it just makes me smile. Nonstop. That is where I find myself mostly these weeks leading up to her birth. Smiling nonstop. Giddy all the time.

It is now January 2015, and we have around two months until our little girl arrives. We are walking in faith and believing that this process will be smooth and that God's hand will be on it all. It is a balance of guarding our hearts, knowing that our birth mom could choose to keep the baby at any point. I just don't think it is possible to find a balance, even though that is what we are seeking. How can you allow yourself to be excited while so much could happen to deter the process? So, we choose to believe. We believe God has brought us to this point and that He will be faithful.

Adoption Pregnancy

We are choosing to celebrate and be joyful during this "adoption pregnancy." I will never forget Josh coming home from work one day and talking about our adoption pregnancy. Here's what happened:

> *I am at home cleaning the house and Josh walks in early. I can always tell when he has something he really wants to talk about. He comes up, grabs me with an intense hug and says, "I need to talk to you about something." I immediately think, "Oh gosh, what is it? What happened?" I thought he had broken something or sold something I didn't want him too (This has happened before as I am married to an entrepreneur). He says, "I want you to experience pregnancy and I have to allow you to do so." Immediately, the tears come. They are free flowing and they won't stop. He continued to explain to me that it is his personality to not let people know*

certain things, or to worry about a failed adoption, but if we did that, then we would not experience what some couples do who are pregnant. Obviously, some couples miscarry or have a stillbirth, and that is completely devastating, and that might happen to us to in this adoption. But he keeps saying that he is sorry for not letting me experience it thus far, and from this point forward, it is his mission to allow me to experience pregnancy. This is our adoption pregnancy."

So, here we are experiencing our adoption pregnancy. We have three months of pregnancy instead of the typical nine months, but we are enjoying every minute of it. We are baby registering, dreaming about nurseries, picturing what she will look like- the whole nine yards. But until Josh had given me that clearance, I was walking somewhat in fear, and now I am walking completely in faith, trusting Jesus every step of the way. He will give me the desires of my heart, even if He had to change them first. And I am so thankful He did.

I'm determined to enjoy the waiting in life. I don't want to be one of those people who wishes the weeks away to get to the weekend. I don't want to be one of those people who is miserable unless on vacation. I don't want to be one of those people who isn't happy unless or until I have a baby. I want to enjoy this season of waiting. I want to enjoy the "in- betweens."

After all, life happens in the in-betweens. Life happens in the waiting. I don't want to miss life because of my impatience. I don't want you to either. Waiting builds trust, and we are trusting Jesus wholeheartedly. Will you trust Him with me?

I didn't want to end this book with the fairy-tale ending of us bringing home our baby. Because that isn't real life. After we bring our baby home, we will have struggles then. That is a little thing called life. I wanted to end with us still trusting, still waiting, still believing when something is yet to be fulfilled. That is where we grow. That is when our, "What if", perspective changes.

What if God is having you go through whatever it is your struggling with to bring you a joy indescribable. To let you experience abundant life. To grow your faith, your character, your trust in Him. It's not fun, and I won't even say parts of it are worth it, but it can bring you to a place with God, with your spouse, and with your children that may not have been experienced any other way.

For me, I've realized that the most painful, most terrible parts of my life have aided in creating the most beautiful parts. It is in the waiting where I realize God's sovereignty reigns over all. It's in the waiting where I realize I really have no control over my life, so why try to control it? It's in the waiting where I realize that infertility led me to adoption. It's in the waiting where I realize that God has planned out every part of my life before I took my first breath. It's it the waiting where I realize that cancer, yes, cancer, made me a mommy.

Here is a photo from one of her ultrasounds. Our sweet
Genevieve Rose.

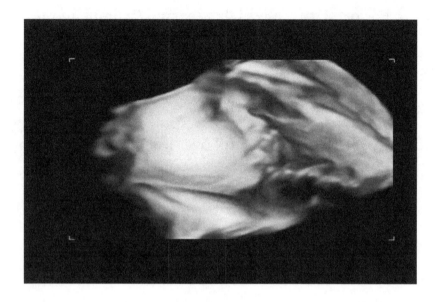

Acknowledgements

This book started when I began to realize that this child we are now awaiting became ours partially through cancer. How could something so terrible like cancer yield something so incredibly miraculous, like our first-born child? It still blows my mind. God has placed many people in my life who have helped me through this cancer journey and now the journey to mommy hood. I do not have the space to thank each and every person, but I will thank those who have played an integral part in this writing process.

Josh...I love you. Who would have ever thought I would be writing a book like this? Not exactly how we saw our lives together when we said, "I do" in 2006. But, you have walked this journey with me in stride. I love doing life with you. Thank you for loving me through cancer and infertility and always viewing our battles as "ours." You are the best of the best. To the man who kissed my mastectomy scars upon first seeing them, I adore you. Thank you for helping me through these last 3 1/2 years and making this book a reality. Any part of me that is good is because of you.

Mom...Thank you for being willing to learn with us throughout this process. It has been a hard road, and I cannot imagine being in your shoes. Thank you for loving us so well, and always being willing to help in any way. I know you are one of my biggest cheerleaders! Thank you for your belief in me and help in this writing process. I love you dearly.

Ms. Renea...I am thankful to have you as my mother-in-law and friend. Thank you for being the mom you are to Josh and hurting with us as we hurt. I know this whole journey has been difficult, yet you still find time to encourage me and offer the world to me. I love you and am so grateful for your help with the completion of this book.

Lauren...my beyond faithful friend, I am forever indebted to you. You have walked by my side through cancer, helped me finish my PhD, counseled me through infertility, and now you are helping throw my baby shower. I love you. You are an inspiration to me!

Christi and Erin...my sweet friends and prayer warriors, thank you for constantly lifting me up both in prayer and inspirit. As you experienced pregnancy during my infertility, you approached it in a way that I am forever grateful for. Your compassion and selflessness toward me has forever impacted my life. I love you.

Jessica, Rachel, Alicia, Ainsley, Kelly, Margot, and Katie...Thank you for loving me so well. I consider you all my sisters, and I could write pages about each one of you! Thank you for always supporting me and seeing the best in me. Thank you for having faith when I did not and praying me through these past 3 1/2 years. I have the best sisters in the world.

Mr. Joey and Mr. Terry...I am incredibly blessed to have you as my stepfather and father-in-law. I have never questioned your love and care for me throughout this process. Thank you for allowing your wives to go above and beyond for me during this journey. I know it was a sacrifice, and I am forever indebted. You are incredibly loved!

My amazing Family Church family...You have wept with me and rejoiced with me through every part of this journey. Thank you for your support- emotionally, financially, spiritually and holding our arms up when we did not have the strength to do it ourselves. We are incredibly blessed with a church family who is the "church" in every sense of the word. I love you all!

My sweet, beautiful, Genevieve Rose...You, my love, are the inspiration behind this book. I have yet to meet you, but I love you with my whole heart. God has amazing plans for your life, and I can't wait to watch it all unfold from the front row. You are precious to us, baby girl. Just a few more months until I see your beautiful face.

Jesus Christ...you are the reason I am here writing this book. I praise you for saving my life and giving me purpose in life. You are my healer, my restorer, my promise keeper, my heavenly father, my everything. Without you, I am nothing, and this book would be nothing. Thank you for blessing the writing and completion of this book. I pray that many would come to know you as I tell this story. This story is *your* story. I love you Jesus.

Healing Scriptures

Exodus 15:26 Amplified Bible (AMP)

"If you will diligently hearken to the voice of the Lord your God and will do what is right in His sight, and will listen to and obey His commandments and keep all His statutes, I will put none of the diseases upon you which I brought upon the Egyptians, for I am the Lord Who heals you."

Exodus 23:25 Amplified Bible (AMP)

"You shall serve the Lord your God; He shall bless your bread and water, and I will take sickness from your midst."

Deuteronomy 7:15 Amplified Bible (AMP)

"And the Lord will take away from you all sickness, and none of the evil diseases of Egypt which you knew will He put upon you, but will lay them upon all who hate you."

Deuteronomy 28:1-2 Amplified Bible (AMP)

"If You will listen diligently to the voice of the Lord your God, being watchful to do all His commandments which I command you this day, the Lord your God will set you high above all the nations of the earth. And all these blessings shall come upon you and overtake you if you heed the voice of the Lord your God."

Deuteronomy 30:19-20 Amplified Bible (AMP)

"I call heaven and earth to witness this day against you that I have set before your life and death, the blessings and the curses; therefore choose life, that you and your descendants may live and may love the Lord your God, obey His voice, and cling to Him. For He is your life and the length of your days, that you may dwell in the land which the Lord swore to give to your fathers, to Abraham, Isaac, and Jacob."

Joshua 21:45 God's Word Translation

"Every single good promise that the Lord had given the nation of Israel came true."

1 Kings 8:56 Amplified Bible (AMP)

"Blessed be the Lord, Who has given rest to His people Israel, according to all that He promised. Not one word has failed of all His good promise which He promised through Moses His servant."

Psalm 89:34 God's Word Translation

"My covenant will I not break, nor alter the thing that is gone out of my lips."

Psalm 91:16 Amplified Bible (AMP)

"With long life will I satisfy him and show him My salvation."

Psalm 103:3 Amplified Bible (AMP)

"Who forgives [every one of] all your iniquities, Who heals [each one of] all your diseases..."

Psalm 105:37 King James Version

"He brought them forth also with silver and gold: and there was not one feeble person among their tribes."

Psalm 107:20 Amplified Bible (AMP)

"He sends forth His word and heals them and rescues them from the pit and destruction."

Psalm 118:17 Amplified Bible (AMP)

"I shall not die but live, and shall declare the works and recount the illustrious acts of the Lord."

Proverbs 3:5-6 God's Word Translation

"Trust the Lord with all your heart, and do not rely on your own understanding. In all your ways acknowledge Him, and He will make your paths smooth."

Proverbs 4:20-23 Amplified Bible (AMP)

"My son, attend to my words; consent and submit to my sayings. Let them not depart from your sight; keep them in the center of your heart. For they are life to those who find them, healing and health to all their flesh. Keep and guard your heart with all vigilance and above all that you guard, for out of it flow the springs of life."

Isaiah 41:10, 13 Amplified Bible (AMP)

"Fear not [there is nothing to fear], for I am with you; do

not look around you in terror and be dismayed, for I am your God. I will strengthen and harden you to difficulties, yes, I will help you; yes, I will hold you up and retain you with My [victorious] right hand of righteousness and justice. For I the Lord your God hold your right hand; I am the Lord, Who says to you, Fear not; I will help you!"

Isaiah 43:25, 26 Amplified Bible (AMP)
"I, even I, am He Who blots out and cancels your transgressions, for My own sake, and I will not remember your sins. Put Me in remembrance [remind Me of your merits]; let us plead and argue together. Set forth your case, that you may be justified (proved right)."

Isaiah 53:4-5 Amplified Bible (AMP)
"Surely He has borne our griefs (sicknesses, weaknesses, and distresses) and carried our sorrows and pains [of punishment], yet we [ignorantly] considered Him stricken, smitten, and afflicted by God [as if with leprosy]. But He was wounded for our transgressions, He was bruised for our guilt and iniquities; the chastisement [needful to obtain] peace and well-being for us was upon

213

Him, and with the stripes [that wounded] Him we are healed and made whole."

Jeremiah 1:12 Amplified Bible (AMP)

"Then said the Lord to me, you have seen well, for I am alert and active, watching over My word to perform it."

Jeremiah 30:17 Amplified Bible (AMP)

"For I will restore health to you, and I will heal your wounds, says the Lord, because they have called you an outcast, saying, this is Zion, whom no one seeks after and for whom no one cares!"

Hosea 4:6 Amplified Bible (AMP)

"My people are destroyed for lack of knowledge; because you [the priestly nation] have rejected knowledge, I will also reject you that you shall be no priest to Me; seeing you have forgotten the law of your God, I will also forget your children."

Joel 3:10 Amplified Bible (AMP)

"Beat your plowshares into swords, and your pruning

hooks into spears; let the weak say, I am strong [a warrior]!"

Nahum 1:7, 9 Amplified Bible (AMP)
"The Lord is good, a Strength and Stronghold in the day of trouble; He knows (recognizes, has knowledge of, and understands) those who take refuge and trust in Him. What do you devise and [how mad is your attempt to] plot against the Lord? He will make a full end [of Nineveh]; affliction [which My people shall suffer from Assyria] shall not rise up the second time."

Matthew 8:2-3 Amplified Bible (AMP) "And behold, a leper came up to Him and, prostrating himself, worshiped Him, saying, Lord, if You are willing, You are able to cleanse me by curing me. And He reached out His hand and touched him, saying, I am willing; be cleansed by being cured. And instantly his leprosy was cured and cleansed."

Matthew 8:17 Amplified Bible (AMP)
"And thus He fulfilled what was spoken by the prophet

Isaiah, He Himself took [in order to carry away] our weaknesses and infirmities and bore away our diseases."

Matthew 18:18-20 Amplified Bible (AMP)
"Truly I tell you, whatever you forbid and declare to be improper and unlawful on earth must be what is already forbidden in heaven, and whatever you permit and declare proper and lawful on earth must be what is already permitted in heaven. Again I tell you, if two of you on earth agree (harmonize together, make a symphony together) about whatever [anything and everything] they may ask, it will come to pass and be done for them by My Father in heaven. For wherever two or three are gathered (drawn together as My followers) in (into) My name, there I am in the midst of them."

Matthew 21:21 Amplified Bible (AMP)
"And Jesus answered them, Truly I say to you, if you have faith (a firm relying trust) and do not doubt, you will not only do what has been done to the fig tree, but even if you say to this mountain, Be taken up and cast into the sea, it will be done."

Mark 11:23-24 Amplified Bible (AMP)

"Truly I tell you, whoever says to this mountain, be lifted up and thrown into the sea! And does not doubt at all in his heart but believes that what he says will take place, it will be done for him. For this reason I am telling you, whatever you ask for in prayer, believe (trust and be confident) that it is granted to you, and you will [get it]."

Mark 16:18 Amplified Bible (AMP)

"They will pick up serpents; and [even] if they drink anything deadly, it will not hurt them; they will lay their hands on the sick, and they will get well."

Luke 10:19 Amplified Bible (AMP) 198

"Behold! I have given you authority and power to trample upon serpents and scorpions, and [physical and mental strength and ability] over all the power that the enemy [possesses]; and nothing shall in any way harm you."

John 9:31 Amplified Bible (AMP)

"We know that God does not listen to sinners; but if

anyone is God-fearing and a worshiper of Him and does His will, He listens to him."

John 10:10 Amplified Bible (AMP)
"The thief comes only in order to steal and kill and destroy. I came that they may have and enjoy life, and have it in abundance (to the full, till it overflows)."

Romans 4:19-21 Amplified Bible (AMP)
"He did not weaken in faith when he considered the [utter] impotence of his own body, which was as good as dead because he was about a hundred years old, or [when he considered] the barrenness of Sarah's [deadened] womb. No unbelief or distrust made him waver (doubtingly question) concerning the promise of God, but he grew strong and was empowered by faith as he gave praise and glory to God, fully satisfied and assured that God was able and mighty to keep His word and to do what He had promised."

Romans 8:11 Amplified Bible (AMP)
"And if the Spirit of Him Who raised up Jesus from the dead dwells in you, [then] He Who raised up Christ Jesus

from the dead will also restore to life your mortal (short-lived, perishable) bodies through His Spirit Who dwells in you."

2 Corinthians 1:20 Amplified Bible (AMP)

"For as many as are the promises of God, they all find their Yes [answer] in Him [Christ]. For this reason we also utter the Amen (so be it) to God through Him [in His Person and by His agency] to the glory of God."

2 Corinthians 10:3-5 Amplified Bible (AMP)

"For though we walk (live) in the flesh, we are not carrying on our warfare according to the flesh and using mere human weapons. For the weapons of our warfare are not physical [weapons of flesh and blood], but they are mighty before God for the overthrow and destruction of strongholds, [Inasmuch as we] refute arguments and theories and reasonings and every proud and lofty thing that sets itself up against the [true] knowledge of God; and we lead every thought and purpose away captive into the obedience of Christ (the Messiah, the Anointed One)"

Galatians 3:13 Amplified Bible (AMP)

"Christ purchased our freedom [redeeming us] from the curse (doom) of the Law [and its condemnation] by [Himself] becoming a curse for us, for it is written [in the Scriptures], Cursed is everyone who hangs on a tree (is crucified)"

Ephesians 6:10-17 Amplified Bible (AMP)

"In conclusion, be strong in the Lord [be empowered through your union with Him]; draw your strength from Him [that strength which His boundless might provides]. Put on God's whole armor [the armor of a heavy-armed soldier which God supplies], that you may be able successfully to stand up against [all] the strategies and the deceits of the devil. For we are not wrestling with flesh and blood [contending only with physical opponents], but against the despotisms, against the powers, against [the master spirits who are] the world rulers of this present darkness, against the spirit forces of wickedness in the heavenly (supernatural) sphere. Therefore put on God's complete armor, that you may be able to resist and stand your ground on the evil day [of danger], and, having done all [the crisis demands], to stand [firmly in your place]. Stand therefore [hold your ground], having tightened the belt of truth around your loins and having put on the breastplate of integrity and of moral rectitude and right standing with God, And having shod your feet in preparation [to face the enemy with the firm-footed stability, the promptness, and the readiness produced by the good news] of the Gospel of peace. Lift up over all the [covering] shield of saving faith, upon which you can quench all the flaming missiles of the wicked [one]. And take the helmet of salvation and the sword that the Spirit wields, which is the Word of God."

Philippians 1:6 Amplified Bible (AMP)
"And I am convinced and sure of this very thing, that He who began a good work in you will continue until the day of Jesus Christ [right up to the time of His return], developing [that good work] and perfecting and bringing it to full completion in you."

Philippians 2:13 Amplified Bible (AMP)
"[Not in your own strength] for it is God who is all the while effectually at work in you [energizing and creating

in you the power and desire], both to will and to work for His good pleasure and satisfaction and delight."

Philippians 4:6-8 Amplified Bible (AMP)
"Do not fret or have any anxiety about anything, but in every circumstance and in everything, by prayer and petition (definite requests), with thanksgiving, continue to make your wants known to God. And God's peace [shall be yours, that tranquil state of a soul assured of its salvation through Christ, and so fearing nothing from God and being content with its earthly lot of whatever sort that is, that peace] which transcends all understanding shall garrison and mount guard over your hearts and minds in Christ Jesus. For the rest, brethren, whatever is true, whatever is worthy of reverence and is honorable and seemly, whatever is just, whatever is pure, whatever is lovely and lovable, whatever is kind and winsome and gracious, if there is any virtue and excellence, if there is anything worthy of praise, think on and weigh and take account of these things [fix your minds on them]."

2 Timothy 1:7 Amplified Bible (AMP)

"For God did not give us a spirit of timidity (of cowardice, of craven and cringing and fawning fear), but [He has given us a spirit] of power and of love and of calm and well- balanced mind and discipline and self-control."

Hebrews 10:23, 25 Amplified Bible (AMP)
"So let us seize and hold fast and retain without wavering the hope we cherish and confess and our acknowledgment of it, for He who promised is reliable (sure) and faithful to His word. Not forsaking or neglecting to assemble together [as believers], as is the habit of some people, but admonishing (warning, urging, and encouraging) one another, and all the more faithfully as you see the day approaching."

Hebrews 10:35 Amplified Bible (AMP)
"Do not, therefore, fling away your fearless confidence, for it carries a great and glorious compensation of reward."

Hebrews 11:11 Amplified Bible (AMP)
"Because of faith also Sarah herself received physical

power to conceive a child, even when she was long past the age for it, because she considered [God] who had given her the promise to be reliable and trustworthy and true to His word."

Hebrews 13:8 Amplified Bible (AMP)
"Jesus Christ (the Messiah) is [always] the same, yesterday, today, [yes] and forever (to the ages)."

James 1:5 Amplified Bible (AMP)
"If any of you is deficient in wisdom, let him ask of the giving God [who gives] to everyone liberally and ungrudgingly, without reproaching or faultfinding, and it will be given him."

James 3:17 Amplified Bible (AMP)
"But the wisdom from above is first of all pure (undefiled); then it is peace-loving, courteous (considerate, gentle). [It is willing to] yield to reason, full of compassion and good fruits; it is wholehearted and straightforward, impartial and unfeigned (free from doubts, wavering, and insincerity)."

James 4:7-8 Amplified Bible (AMP)

"So be subject to God. Resist the devil [stand firm against him], and he will flee from you. Come close to God and He will come close to you. [Recognize that you are] sinners, get your soiled hands clean; [realize that you have been disloyal] wavering individuals with divided interests, and purify your hearts [of your spiritual adultery]."

James 5:14-15 Amplified Bible (AMP)

"Is anyone among you sick? He should call in the church elders (the spiritual guides). And they should pray over him, anointing him with oil in the Lord's name. And the prayer [that is] of faith will save him who is sick, and the Lord will restore him; and if he has committed sins, he will be forgiven."

1 Peter 2:24 Amplified Bible (AMP)

"He personally bore our sins in His [own] body on the tree [as on an altar and offered Himself on it], that we might die (cease to exist) to sin and live to righteousness. By His wounds you have been healed."

1 Peter 5:7-9 Amplified Bible (AMP)

"Casting the whole of your care [all your anxieties, all your worries, all your concerns, once and for all] on Him, for He cares for you affectionately and cares about you watchfully. Be well balanced (temperate, sober of mind), be vigilant and cautious at all times; for that enemy of yours, the devil, roams around like a lion roaring in fierce hunger, seeking someone to seize upon and devour. Withstand him; be firm in faith [against his onset–rooted, established, strong, immovable, and determined], knowing that the same (identical) sufferings are appointed to your brotherhood (the whole body of Christians) throughout the world."

1 John 3:21-22 Amplified Bible (AMP)

"And, beloved, if our consciences (our hearts) do not accuse us [if they do not make us feel guilty and condemn us], we have confidence (complete assurance and boldness) before God, and we receive from Him whatever we ask, because we [watchfully] obey His orders [observe His suggestions and injunctions, follow His plan for us] and [habitually] practice what is pleasing to Him."

1 John 5:14-15 Amplified Bible (AMP)

"And this is the confidence (the assurance, the privilege of boldness) which we have in Him: [we are sure] that if we ask anything (make any request) according to His will (in agreement with His own plan), He listens to and hears us. And if (since) we [positively] know that He listens to us in whatever we ask, we also know [with settled and absolute knowledge] that we have [granted us as our present possessions] the requests made of Him."

3 John 1:2 Amplified Bible (AMP)

"Beloved, I pray that you may prosper in every way and [that your body] may keep well, even as [I know] your soul keeps well and prospers."

Revelation 12:11 Amplified Bible (AMP)

"And they have overcome (conquered) him by means of the blood of the Lamb and by the utterance of their testimony, for they did not love and cling to life even when faced with death [holding their lives cheap until they had to die for their witnessing].

More Scriptures from the New King James Translation:

"My son, give attention to my words; Incline your ear to my sayings. Do not let them depart from your eyes; Keep them in the midst of your heart. For they are life to those who find them, And health to all their flesh." (Prov 4:20-22 NKJV)

"God's word will not fail. Not a word failed of any good thing which the Lord had spoken to the house of Israel. All came to pass." (Josh 21:45 NKJV)

"God's will — healing– is working in you. For it is God who works in you both to will and to do for His good pleasure." (Phil 2:13 NKJV)

"But if the Spirit of Him who raised Jesus from the dead dwells in you, He who raised Christ from the dead will also give life to your mortal bodies through His Spirit who dwells in you." (Rom 8:11 NKJV)

"For all the promises of God in Him are Yes, and in Him Amen, to the glory of God through us." (2 Cor 1:20 NKJV)

"And behold, a leper came and worshipped Him, saying, "Lord, if You are willing, You can make me clean. Then Jesus put out His hand and touched him, saying, "I am willing; be cleansed." Immediately his leprosy was cleansed." (Mat 8:2-3 NKJV)

"And said, "If you diligently heed the voice of the LORD your God and do what is right in His sight, give ear to His commandments and keep all His statutes, I will put none of the diseases on you which I have brought on the Egyptians. For I am the LORD who heals you." (Exo 15:26 NKJV)

"So you shall serve the LORD your God, and He will bless your bread and your water. And I will take sickness away from the midst of you." (Exo 23:25 NKJV)

"And the LORD will take away from you all sickness, and will afflict you with none of the terrible diseases of Egypt which you have known, but will lay them on all those who hate you." (Deu 7:15 NKJV)

"Bring all the tithes into the storehouse, That there may be food in My house, And try Me now in this," Says the LORD of hosts, "If I will not open for you the windows of heaven And pour out for you such blessing That there will not be room enough to receive it. (Mal 3:10 NKJV)

"Bless the LORD, O my soul; And all that is within me, bless His holy name. Bless the LORD, O my soul, And forget not all His benefits: Who forgives all your iniquities, Who heals all your diseases, Who redeems your life from destruction, Who crowns you with lovingkindness and tender mercies, Who satisfies your mouth with good things, So that your youth is renewed like the eagle's." (Psa 103:1-5 NKJV)

"He sent His word and healed them, And delivered them from their destructions." (Psa 107:20 NKJV)

" I shall not die, but live, And declare the works of the LORD." (Psa 118:17 NKJV)

"I call heaven and earth as witnesses today against you, that I have set before you life and death, blessing and cursing; therefore choose life, that both you and your descendants may live;" (Deu 30:19 NKJV)

"With long life I will satisfy him, And show him My salvation." (Psa 91:16 NKJV)

"But He was wounded for our transgressions, He was bruised for our iniquities; The chastisement for our peace was upon Him, And by His stripes we are healed." (Isa 53:5 NKJV)

"For I will restore health to you And heal you of your wounds,' says the LORD, 'Because they called you an outcast saying: "This is Zion; No one seeks her."' (Jer 30:17 NKJV)

"Assuredly, I say to you, whatever you bind on earth will be bound in heaven, and whatever you loose on earth will be loosed in heaven." (Mat 18:18 NKJV)

Again I say to you that if two of you agree on earth concerning anything that they ask, it will be done for them by My Father in heaven." (Mat 18:19 NKJV)

"So Jesus answered and said to them, "Have faith in God. "For assuredly, I say to you, whoever says to this mountain, 'Be removed and be cast into the sea,' and does not doubt in his heart, but believes that those things he says will be done, he will have whatever he says."(Mark 11:22-23 NKJV)

"Therefore I say to you, whatever things you ask when you pray, believe that you receive them, and you will have them." (Mark 11:24 NKJV)

"Even I, am He who blots out your transgressions for My own sake; And I will not remember your sins. Put Me in remembrance; Let us contend together; State your case, that you may be acquitted." (Isa 43:25-26 NKJV)

"And these signs will follow those who believe: In My name they will cast out demons; they will speak with new tongues; "they will take up serpents; and if they drink anything deadly, it will by no means hurt them; they will lay hands on the sick, and they will recover." (Mark 16:17-18 NKJV)

"Now we know that God does not hear sinners; but if anyone is a worshiper of God and does His will, He hears him." (John 9:31 NKJV)

"The thief does not come except to steal, and to kill, and to destroy. I have come that they may have life, and that they may have it more abundantly." (John 10:10 NKJV)

"Christ has redeemed us from the curse of the law, having become a curse for us (for it is written, "Cursed is everyone who hangs on a tree"), that the blessing of Abraham might come upon the Gentiles in Christ Jesus, that we might receive the promise of the Spirit through faith." (Gal 3:13-14 NKJV)

"Let us hold fast the confession of our hope without wavering, for He who promised is faithful." (Heb 10:23 NKJV)

"Therefore do not cast away your confidence, which has great reward." (Heb 10:35 NKJV)

".... Let the weak say, 'I am strong.'" (Joel 3:10 NKJV)

"Jesus Christ is the same yesterday, today, and forever." (Heb 13:8 NKJV)

"Beloved, I wish above all things that thou mayest prosper and be in health, even as thy soul prospereth." (3 John 1:2 KJV)

"Is anyone among you sick? Let him call for the elders of the church, and let them pray over him, anointing him with oil in the name of the Lord. And the prayer of faith will save the sick, and the Lord will raise him up. And if he has committed sins, he will be forgiven. (James 5:14-15 NKJV)

"Who Himself bore our sins in His own body on the tree, that we, having died to sins, might live for righteousness; by whose stripes you were healed." (1 Pet 2:24 NKJV)

"Now this is the confidence that we have in Him, that if we ask anything according to His will, He hears us. And if we know that He hears us, whatever we ask, we know that we have the petitions that we have asked of Him." (1 John 5:14- 15 NKJV)

"Beloved, if our heart does not condemn us, we have confidence toward God. And whatever we ask we receive from Him, because we keep His commandments and do those things that are pleasing in His sight." (1 John 3:21-22 NKJV)

"For God has not given us a spirit of fear, but of power and of love and of a sound mind." (2 Tim 1:7 NKJV)

"For the weapons of our warfare are not carnal but mighty in God for pulling down strongholds, casting down arguments and every high thing that exalts itself against the knowledge of God, bringing every thought into captivity to the obedience of Christ" (2 Cor 10:4-5 NKJV)

"Finally, my brethren, be strong in the Lord and in the power of His might. Put on the whole armor of God, that you may be able to stand against the wiles of the devil. For we do not wrestle against flesh and blood, but against principalities, against powers, against the rulers of the darkness of this age, against spiritual hosts of wickedness in the heavenly places. Therefore take up the whole armor of God, that you may be able to withstand in the evil day, and having done all, to stand. Stand therefore, having girded your waist with truth, having put on the breastplate of righteousness, and having shod your feet with the preparation of the gospel of peace; above all, taking the shield of faith with which you will be able to quench all the fiery darts of the wicked one. And take the helmet of salvation, and the sword of the Spirit, which is the word of God; (Eph 6:10-17 NKJV)

"And they overcame him by the blood of the Lamb and by the word of their testimony, and they did not love their lives to the death." (Rev 12:11 NKJV)

"What do you conspire against the LORD? He will make an utter end of it. Affliction will not rise up a second time." (Nahum 1:9 NKJV)

My Diet

The battle

From the moment I was diagnosed, I was scared to eat. I was scared to drink. In my mind, I felt like anything I would put in my body could make the cancer grow! It was a place of bondage for me, that thankfully I am somewhat out of now.

My amazing mother-in-law, along with several others have helped me in trying to change my diet and eat foods that can make me as healthy as possible. What I am sharing with you is not an "anti-cancer" diet or even foods that can cure cancer, but simply diet choices that I've made to help me get and stay as healthy as possible.

If anyone knows me, you know I am a HUGE foodie. I love food. Pasta, pizza, mexican, ice cream, sweets...really healthy food. Yeah, right:) So, this undertaking of changing my diet was literally a 180! Listed below are the diet changes that I have tried to stick to, along with some recipes that somewhat satisfy my sweet tooth.

I do believe that God gave us so many natural things to keep us healthy and strong. I know He desires for me to be healthy...that my body is His temple, and I am committed to taking care of it. This has been a lifestyle change for me. One that has affected my husband and a diet that I hope and pray to raise my children up in. I desire for them to live long, healthy lives as well! We do somewhat have control over that with our diets.

So...here are my basic restrictions

- Little to no bread. If I ever eat bread, I will do whole wheat or whole wheat tortillas, but I really don't eat bread at all.

- Little to no sugar. I try to stay away from sugar totally, outside of fruits and other foods with naturally occurring sugar.

- No cream or dairy products. I do eat eggs and Unsweetened Vanilla Almond milk.

- I don't eat any red meat, except for deer meat, as it is very lean. And it comes from the deer that my husband and I kill, so I know more about it:)

- I try to stay away from all processed food. If I do eat something processed, I try to eat organically.

So, what do I eat?

Oatmeal

Organic cereals with little sugar Fish, chicken, deer meat

Veggies

Fruit

Eggs

Brown Rice

Unsweetened vanilla almond milk Fresh Juice

Sweet potatoes

Nuts (mainly almonds and walnuts) Raisins

Lots of salads

Avocado

Black beans

Kind bars

Larabars (certain ones)

Almond butter

Unsweetened coconut

Olive oil

Honey and stevia for sweeteners

Eating healthy is expensive!!!

I've read blogs that say that eating healthy is just as costly as eating unhealthy, and I just haven't found that to be the case. It is so much more expensive, at least for us. Our grocery bill has nearly tripled each month since my diet changes. Thank the Lord for those who continue to give to us.

I have to see it as an investment. What better thing to invest in outside of the kingdom of God? My temple...my husband's temple...our future children's bodies. I am such a tight wad, so to see that money going to food and then paying for a gym membership- it pains me! But, I have to remind myself that it is an investment. In my health, and ultimately my life.

Please share!

As I've said before, I know that everything I've been through has not been in vain. I believe that each part of my journey has brought me closer to God and has brought others closer to Him too. We can all benefit from keeping our bodies healthy.

I am working on a recipe book, but if you need any suggestions before that is up and running, please feel free to reach me via my email or social media, which is listed at the end of this book.

1 Corinthians 6: 19-20 "Don't you realize that your body is the temple of the Holy Spirit, who lives in you and was given to you by God? You do not belong to yourself, for God bought you with a high price. So you must honor God with your body."

Cancer Caretaking

Through our journey of my healing from breast cancer, we have gotten a front-seat view of what caretaking is all about. Not only has my husband been the best caretaker I could have ever imagined, but we've had others take care of us in huge ways. We thought we would share some things that others have done to help us, or suggestions of some things to do when you know someone who has been diagnosed with cancer. These are not suggestions for cancer caretaking from MD Anderson, or from Susan G. Komen, these are simply homemade suggestions from Josh and Aly Taylor. We wanted to make that clear. We have been BEYOND blessed to have had amazing caretaking.

1.) Pray specifically for your loved one. A great idea is to write out a prayer. **Send it in a text, a card, or make a craft. **I know for me, prayer is the thing that gave me the most hope.

2.) Offer to do **_specific_ things**. So often people ask,

"What can I do?" or "Let me know if I can do anything." Truthfully, I really didn't know of what to tell others to do. The ones who helped the most asked, "What can I bring you for supper?," or "I dropped you some juice at the front door," or "Please send me your grocery list and I will drop off your groceries on your front porch."

3.) Be **positive.** So many people with good intentions want to talk with one diagnosed with cancer, by telling a story of someone they knew with cancer. A parent, aunt, relative, friend...Please be wise. Cancer patients are so fragile (I still am) and do not need to hear of someone who has died or had a terrible time with cancer. Tell a story of someone who know who was miraculously healed or has been a survivor for 20+ years. I know intentions are always good, but cancer patients need to hear positive stories.

4.) Make a list of scriptures on healing and send it to your loved one. Commit to pray those verses over your loved one. Make it **personal** and put their name in the verses. As I've shared before, I had 2 groups of people who did this for me and it was better than any book anyone gave me.

5.) Find out what someone **enjoys** and send them a goody basket. Check with a relative about their dietary needs and send them a basket with their favorite foods, magazines, games etc... Include a note about praying for joy as they enjoy their goody basket.

6.) **Expect** healing. When you talk to someone with cancer, and you know they have a check-up, say, "Can't wait to hear the good news," or "This will all be behind you so soon," or "What an incredible testimony you will have." It was comments like these that would bring me to tears so often. These words gave me hope, because so many were scared to say them. Don't be scared. Believe what you say and say it in faith. It may increase the one who needs faith desperately.

7.) Serve your loved one in the easiest way possible **for them**. I call this "the porch concept." Leave things on the porch! I know sometimes for me, I may not have wanted someone to bring me food because I was embarrassed of the way I looked. What helped me were those who said, "I dropped off food at your front door," or someone who asked me to leave my laundry on my front porch and they would wash and bring it back to me. Ask your loved one if they would leave their key somewhere easy for you to find so you can have someone clean their house. Whatever the way you serve...make it as easy on your loved one as possible and be specific!

8.) Be **generous**. If it was not for the generosity of others, I truly do not know where Josh and I would be financially. At this point, we've been to Houston over 60 times. We needed gas and food,. We had to pay medical bills, house bills, hotel rooms...We had to take off work...if cancer wasn't overwhelming enough, financially it could have been horrible. But, people were generous. So many times, we would receive a check that would literally drop us to our knees. We have a few incredible people that continue to give. It is not the money. It is what the money represents- Peace. Sending money is an incredible gift. Send a note with it and commit to pray.

9.) Find out their **needs**! I guess this goes back to being specific. We had someone pay for our rental car, our gas, make me juice, make me healthy meals, people that send us whole foods gift cards, a plane ride to Houston. The list goes on and on. These generous people found out what we needed, and simply met the need. If they would have just asked how they could have helped, we probably would have just said, "We will let you know." (which would have probably turned into nothing)

10.) Send books on **healing**. Books were a great gift, as I spent much of my time in a car, and wanting to read rather than watch T.V. and was too weak to really do anything else. Some books were great. Others were not so great. People would get me a book on cancer, and even if the title looked hopeful and good, there were still statistics and parts in the book that would scare me. I found the most helpful books for me were about God's healing; not advances in cancer treatment. Once again- this is just me- your loved one may be different.

11.) Remember that every cancer situation is **different**. Many people shared their stories with us, and so many times it was very helpful; however, sometimes it was wasn't/isn't. Especially people who have a similar to identical diagnosis- many will assume that how one reacts to treatment, emotionally and physically will be the same, and this just isn't the case most of the time. Guard your words, and when you question whether or not to say it, it's probably best not to:)

12.) Use **wisdom** in talking with spouse/family members. I know my husband, mom, and in-laws said that people flooded them with information, and this was good. I know it was overwhelming for them at times too. I know they would say that they would much rather people tell them information than me, but, it is important to know that family members are overwhelmed as well. I would suggest treating the family as the patient! One of the best things that a friend told us was that Josh has had breast cancer. I remember thinking, "What?" He has had it in his own way, and my family has too. It's good to remember that when talking with family members.

13.) Spouse, family members, and friends need to act as **safeguards**. I have had to ask my husband and family multiple times to safeguard me from information. Most of the time, they were wanting to tell me a story of someone who was diagnosed, or some article to read, or a program to watch...which you would think would be good, right? Well, these things said on a day I am struggling can flood me with fearful emotions. So, I have had to be honest with my family and have told them that I need them to be a filter for me. I know this is so hard for my family, but that is just where I find myself most of the time.

14.) **Mail**, email, or text scripture to your loved one. We had a lady who sent me a card in the mail every day, yes EVERY DAY! All it had was a scripture and her name. Every day I looked forward to getting her piece of mail. It reminded me that someone was praying for me every day. Such a simple gesture that I rank as one of the top cancer caretaking things done for me.

15.) Remember that after one is deemed cancer-free, **they are still struggling!** As most of you know, I have struggled way more after cancer than I did before or during. I think people see me with my hair, and going about "normal" life and think I must be in the best spirits having overcome what I did. Am I thankful?! Oh my, yes! But, even functioning is hard at times. All of the things I listed above, I still need NOW. Remember that when your loved one is cancer-free!

Fertility / Motherhood Promises

When I first learned of my cancer diagnosis, my doctor suggested preserving my fertility because undergoing my particular treatment would lower my chance of conception. We felt peace to take steps toward preservation and were heading down that road; however, just a few hours later, she received a report that showed the severity of my cancer. My doctor did not feel comfortable waiting for me to preserve my fertility. She wanted me to start my cancer treatment "last week," but of course the decision remained up to us.

We prayed and felt peace to undergo treatment immediately. This meant that our family's future was at stake. That day and even now, we believe that God protected my womb and my fertility. As we get closer to growing our family, we are meditating on scriptures such as these. We believe that children are a blessing from the

Lord and are expectantly awaiting these precious blessings.

Gen. 1:28 "Then God blessed them and said, "Be fruitful and multiply. Fill the earth and govern it.""

Gen. 3:16 "Then he said to the woman, "I will sharpen the pain of your pregnancy, and in pain you will give birth. And you will desire to control your husband, but he will rule over you."

Gen. 9:1 After the flood God again commanded Noah and his family and said, "Be fruitful, and multiply, and replenish the earth."

Psalm 84: 11 "For the Lord God is our sun and our shield. He gives us grace and glory. The LORD will withhold no good thing from those who do what is right."

Psalm 127: 3-5 "Children are a gift from the Lord; they are a reward from Him. Children born to a young man are like arrows in a warrior's hands. How joyful is the man whose quiver is full of them! He will not be put to shame when he confronts his accusers at the city gates."

Psalm 113: 9 "He gives the childless woman a family, making her a happy mother. Praise the Lord!"

Psalm 128:1-6 "How joyful are those who fear the LORD all who follow His ways! You will enjoy the fruit of your labor. How joyful and prosperous you will be! Your wife will be like a fruitful grapevine, flourishing within your home. Your children will be like vigorous young olive trees as they sit around your table. That is the Lord's blessing for those who fear him."

Gal. 3:9 "Now that you belong to Christ, you are the true children of Abraham. You are his heirs, and now all the promises God gave to him belong to you."

Deut. 7:14 "You shall be blessed above all peoples; there shall not be a male or female barren among you or among your livestock."

Deut. 28: 1-2 "If you fully obey the Lord your God and carefully keep all his commands that I am giving you today, the Lord your God will set you high above all the nations of the world. You will experience all these blessings if you obey the Lord your God."

Deut. 28:11 "Your children and your crops will be blessed. The Lord will give you prosperity in the land he swore to your ancestors to give you, blessing you with many children, numerous livestock, and abundant crops."

Exodus 23:26 "There shall be *no one* miscarrying or barren in your land; I will fulfill the number of your days."

Romans 4:17-18 "Abraham's faith did not weaken, even though he knew that he was too old to be a father at the age of one hundred and that Sarah, his wife, had never been able to have children. He staggered not at the promise of God through unbelief; but was strong in faith, giving glory to God."

Hebrews 11:11 "By faith Sarah herself also received strength to conceive seed, and she bore a child when she was past the age, because she judged Him faithful who had promised"

Genesis 25:21 "Isaac pleaded with the Lord on behalf of his wife, because she was unable to have children. The Lord answered Isaac's prayer, and Rebekah became pregnant with twins."

1 Samuel 1:27 "I prayed for this child, and the Lord has granted me what I asked of Him."

Luke 1:13 "But the angel said to Him, Do not be afraid, Zacharias, for *your prayer is heard*; and your wife Elizabeth will bear you a son, and you shall call his name John. And you will have joy and gladness, and many will rejoice at his birth."

Psalm 139:13 "For You formed my inward parts; You covered me in my mother's womb."

Psalm 139:14 "I will praise You, for I am fearfully and wonderfully made; Marvelous are Your works, And that my soul knows very well."

Psalm 139:15 "You watched me as I was being formed in utter seclusion, as I was woven together in the dark of the womb".

Psalm 22:9-10 "But You are He who took Me out of the womb. You made Me trust while on My mother's breasts. I was cast upon You from birth. From My mother's womb You have been My God."

Isaiah 66:9 "Shall I bring to the birth, and not cause to bring forth? saith the LORD: shall I cause to bring forth, and shut the womb? saith thy God.

Notes

Although few books are literally referenced in this book, there were several books that inspired and brought me to the place of writing this book. The books below helped inspire my writing and I HIGHLY recommend them.

Osteen, D. (1986). *Healed of cancer*. Houston, Tex.: John Osteen.

Ostyn, M. (2014). *Forever mom: What to expect when you're adopting*. Nashville, Tennessee: Thomas Nelson.

Saake, J. (2005). *Hannah's hope: Seeking God's heart in the midst of infertility, miscarriage, and adoption loss*. Colorado Springs, CO: NavPress.

About the Author

Aly Taylor is a wife to Josh and a soon-to-be mommy of her daughter, Genevieve. She is a family therapist and works as a school counselor and online professor. Since diagnosed with breast cancer three and a half years ago, her husband, Josh started a blog, alysfight.com to keep friends and family updated on her cancer treatment. It has since continued to tell her miracle story and encourages others to live a simple life-seeing God in the big miraculous moments, and in the not-so-in-your-face moments.

This is Aly's second book, as she wrote her PhD dissertation that was published in May of 2014. It is entitled: *Breast Cancer at 24: Personal and Familial Experiences of a Breast Cancer Diagnosis and Treatment.* She and her husband, Josh, are working on their first book together, and her third book, entitled *Aly's Fight* where they share the in depth experience of going through cancer together at age 24 and 27.

To those who know her best, Aly is a simple girl who loves Jesus Christ, her family, and struggles with keeping her house tidy, balancing time, and people clipping their nails in public places.

WEBSITE: If you enjoyed *How Cancer Made Me a Mommy,* equip yourself with additional resources at alysfight.com.

SOCIAL MEDIA: Connect with Aly (and Josh), see pictures of her family, and follow her speaking and book schedules:

• BLOG: www.alysfight.com

• FACEBOOK: www.Facebook.com/alysfight

* INSTAGRAM: @alyptaylor

• TWITTER: @alyptaylor

CPSIA information can be obtained
at www.ICGtesting.com
Printed in the USA
BVHW04s2034260718
522793BV00017B/128/P